SEEKING SON LIGHT

Living in the Light of God's Word

BY

REBECCA S. HELTON

Seeking Son Light
Living in the Light of God's Word
by Rebecca S. Helton

Printed in the United States of America

ISBN 9781498406932

www.xulonpress.com

Table of Contents

Section 3:   **The Life of Christ**

Introduction

Several years ago as I was browsing in a bookstore, I literally bumped into a large display containing several stacks of bargain books. Fortunately only one book fell off the table. It looked like a typical novel until I looked more closely. It was actually the contemporary English version of the Bible. Of the dozens of books that were stacked up on that table, this is the only one that fell to the floor and somehow ended up in my hands.

My grandmother taught me at a very early age that the Bible contained a wealth of information and that it told us everything we needed to know in order to live godly lives. As an adult I wanted to feel about the Bible like my grandmother did. I wanted to be able to find the answers to life's questions and to find peace within its pages, but I found it nearly impossible to understand its writings. The King James Version was the only Bible I owned and every time I tried to read it, I quickly became frustrated and put it back on the shelf.

But once I had that contemporary English version of the Bible in my hands, it was as if a veil had been lifted. I spent every available moment with that book and read it from cover to cover. It is difficult to express the excitement and thrill of discovering for oneself the amazing contents of the Bible. It contains history, prophecy, romance and intrigue. Only through its pages can we learn about the very nature of God.

Every new Christian knows the feeling of wanting to share their new found joy with family and friends. And like me, they have probably experienced the lack of responsiveness in those same people. I eventually became aware that whenever I began speaking about the Bible, my friends' eyes would glaze over and they were mentally gone. These were the friends with whom I used to have everything in common but I soon discovered that I was far more interested in the Bible than I was in the latest fashions, newest movies or hottest vacation spots. And that is when I realized that I had changed.

It was unfathomable to me that most people not only did not share my enthusiasm for the Bible, but they had no interest in it whatsoever. I began to research the question, "Are Americans biblically illiterate?" and discovered that the resounding answer is YES! In fact, a recent Barna poll indicated that many adults believe Joan of Arc was Noah's wife, Sodom and Gomorrah were a husband and wife and that the Sermon on the Mount was originally preached by Bill Graham.

At the moment, you might be asking, "So what?" Does it really matter anyway?

It is not surprising that the secular world is not knowledgeable about the Bible, although education in American history, art and culture are incomplete without some understanding of biblical references.

Of greater concern is the fact that many professing Christians are as ignorant of biblical teachings as their secular counterparts. Polls of adults claiming to be Christians indicate that less than half could name the four Gospels, could not identify even two or three of the disciples and, although they claimed to live by the Ten Commandments, they did not know what they were. Many believed that the phrase, "God helps those who help themselves" could be found in the Bible. These are also the people who refuse to believe that a loving God would actually condemn someone to an eternity in hell. For sure, the Bible contains "need to know" information.

This book is my attempt to help biblically illiterate Christians put away their fear of the Bible. Section 1 is titled, "This Book We Call the Bible" and it provides some interesting facts and statistics about the Bible itself. It explains why we can trust the Bible and its teachings. Since the Bible is the foundation upon which our beliefs are based, it is critical that we have a good understanding of exactly what the Bible is, what it is not, and why it is trustworthy. Those who do not have that solid foundation find it very easy to fall away when the going gets tough.

Section 2 is all about the Ten Commandments. A common question many Christians have is whether we have any responsibility to the Ten Commandments today, and the answer is "Yes" and "No". In each lesson in Section 2, I discuss what each of the Commandments meant to the Israelites and what they mean to Christians today.

Section 3 is "The Life of Christ". I want readers to *feel* Him, not just gain an academic understanding of who Jesus is but to really come to know Him as a Person. The lessons in this section show Jesus' humanity as well as His deity.

Finally, let me mention that although I began with the contemporary English version of the Bible, I "graduated" to more scholarly versions: the New International Version (NIV) and the New American Standard Bible (NASB). A true Seeker of Truth will not be content to simply accept another's interpretation of the Bible but will be compelled to discover the ultimate truth for himself. (For more information about Bible versions and translations, refer to Lesson 6 in Section 1).

I hope you enjoy this journey into the Bible and that the true Seeker within you is awakened.

Blessings.
Rebecca Helton

Dedicated to

Dossie Alice Martin

("Grandma Martin" to me)

She introduced me to Jesus Christ when I was just a child and instilled in me a lifelong love for God's Word.

Acknowledgements

In 1 Corinthians 12, the Apostle Paul tells of spiritual gifts: "Now to each one the manifestation of the Spirit is given for the common good." While some may struggle to recognize the gifts they have been given by the Spirit, I recognize that mine is the gift of writing. I am at once humbled and excited that the Spirit has used me to offer a lifeline to those who need a place to start exploring the Bible. I pray that my ministry in literary evangelism will inspire others to allow the Holy Spirit to work through them for the common good.

Many thanks go to my pastor, Dr. Gary E. Gilley of Southern View Chapel in Springfield, Illinois. "Pastor Gary" scrutinized every lesson, both teaching and encouraging me along the way. Because of his careful review and approval of the theological content in this book, I can truly say that every lesson has been "pastor-ized"! I thank God daily that He led me to this wonderful, Bible teaching church. It is filled with men and women who possess a depth of biblical knowledge not seen in most American churches today.

I also want to thank Harold and Ruth Green for their assistance in proof reading my manuscript. They are fellow members of Southern View Chapel and their attention to detail is amazing to me. Their efforts are greatly appreciated.

My sister, Elaine Sosman, assisted me with the project and her help was invaluable. Elaine was my sounding board when I had an idea, my critic when I went astray and my cheerleader when I got it right. And the best part is that we are not only sisters because we were born to the same parents but we are sisters in Christ because we were born again in Him.

Finally, thanks to my husband Ron who took this journey with me. For the past forty years as husband and wife, we have faced every challenge, every sorrow and every joy together. Mere words cannot express my gratitude for his support and encouragement in all that I do. He truly is a gift from God.

Seeking Son Light

Section 1

This Book We Call the Bible

Lesson 1

What is the Bible?

The Bible is nothing less than the key
to our salvation.

Section 1: This Book We Call the Bible
Lesson 1: What is the Bible?

It is appropriate to begin a Bible study with a study of the Bible itself. What is the Bible, really? Is it still important today? How do we know we can trust it? Who wrote it? These are important questions.

The Bible is nothing less than the key to our salvation. *(Romans 1:16)*

The Bible is a unique book. It is the best selling book of all time with an estimated 100 million copies published annually. It was the first book printed on the Gutenberg Press. It is the most translated book in the world and is available in whole or in part to 98 percent of the world's population in a language they can understand.

It contains 66 ancient books and letters that were compiled many centuries ago into the single volume we have today. It was written over a period of about 1,500 years in three languages (Hebrew, Greek and Aramaic) on three continents (Africa, Asia and Europe) by approximately 40 different human authors who ranged from shepherds to kings. And yet it is unified and has complete continuity. The various Bible books are in complete harmony with one another.

It is separated into two major sections. The first is called the Old Testament and this section covers the period of time from creation until about 400 years before Jesus Christ was born. The second section is called the New Testament and it begins with the birth of Jesus Christ.

The word "testament" is actually another word for "covenant" so the Bible tells us of the Old Covenant and the New Covenant.

The Bible is inerrant, meaning that the original manuscripts contained no errors or mistakes. (Psalm 119:160; Proverbs 30:5) Christians believe that it is absolute truth. It is infallible, meaning it is accurate and true in all that it says on matters of faith, morals, the physical world, the universe, history, science and prophecy.

How can any book claim to possess all of these qualities? Because the Bible is not just "any" book. It is the very Word of God. It is His message to us. The Bible is the "inspired" Word of God. Used in this way, the word *inspired* means "God breathed" (2 Timothy 3:16). That is, the message contained in the Bible is from the mouth of God. We cannot know for certain exactly how God's message was transmitted to the people who wrote it down (Exodus 24:4). But being the very creator of the universe, God was certainly capable of placing knowledge and certain truths into the minds of human beings who later wrote these things down. While the message is directly from God, He used human authors to record that message and their individual personalities are evident in their writing. In a real sense, these authors used a ghostwriter: the Holy Ghost! (2 Peter 1:21)

The Bible is unique in another way as well. It is unique in its preservation. Throughout the Middle East and Mediterranean regions, there are thousands of Old Testament documents that are in remarkable agreement with one another. They are also in agreement with the ancient Jewish

Scriptures and the Dead Sea Scrolls that were discovered in Israel in the 1940's. In addition, there are nearly 6,000 New Testament documents in the original Greek form.

No other ancient writing can make claim to so many preserved manuscripts. In fact, the second best preserved ancient writing after the Bible is Homer's *Illiad,* of which there are only 643 remaining documents. None of William Shakespeare's manuscripts are preserved to the present day.

So how can we account for this discrepancy in the number of ancient manuscripts between the Bible and other writings?

It is because the Bible was supernaturally created and supernaturally preserved.

In spite of numerous attempts throughout the centuries to burn, ban, discredit and destroy the Bible, it remains to this day. God's purpose in leaving His written message to us was to provide guidance for godly living until Jesus Christ returns again and nothing will thwart His purpose. Jesus said,

"Heaven and earth will pass away, but My words will not pass away."
(Matthew 24:35)

How the Bible was Compiled

The word "canon" is often used in reference to the list of books that were included in the Bible we use today. The Greek word translated *canon* actually means rule or measuring rod. Christians today can think of it as a standard (*i.e.* measuring rod) that had to be achieved in order for a book to be included in the Bible.

Understanding how the canon came into existence is not necessary for one to achieve salvation, but Christians should have some idea of the process that was used to determine which books could pass the test of authenticity and authority which was the hallmark of inspiration.

There was little question concerning the books that were included in the Old Testament because these books were written by Moses and the other prophets whose authority was never questioned. It is thought that the books were completed by about 420 B.C. and compiled by Ezra and Nehemiah.

However, in order for a book to be accepted into the New Testament canon, it underwent rigorous examination to validate its authorship, inspiration and authority. The answers to the following questions were used to determine a book's "canonicity":

- Was the book apostolic in origin?
- Was the book used and recognized by the churches?
- Did the book teach sound doctrine?

A main goal for establishing the canon was to collect and preserve the writings and teachings of the Apostles, all of whom had died by the end of the first century A.D. The final list of books that passed the test for inclusion in the New Testament was completed early in A.D. 367, although the books themselves were written during the period from about A.D. 50 to A.D. 100. The canon was confirmed at the Council of Carthage in A.D. 397. Once the final list of accepted books was established, it was said that the "canon was closed", meaning that no other books would be accepted as being inspired and therefore worthy of being included in the New Testament.

What became of the books that did not bear the hallmark of inspiration? Many of them are actually included in the modern day Roman Catholic Bibles and they are referred to as the *apocrypha*. They do offer some value in terms of understanding the historical setting and cultural nuances of the day, but they should not be considered to be on the same level as the inspired Scriptures.

Some critics argue that the Bible cannot be considered infallible due to the human involvement in the process of determining which books should be included in it. However, just as the human authors worked under the inspiration and supervision of the Holy Spirit, so too did those involved in determining the Bible canon.

The Bible truly is the Word of God.

LESSON 1 – SUMMARY

READ

Romans 1:16, Psalm 119:160, Proverbs 30:5, 2 Timothy 3:16, Exodus 24:4, 2 Peter 1:21, Matthew 24:35

REFLECT

Why is the Bible a unique book?

_____

_____

_____

What do we mean when we say the Bible is *inspired*?

_____

_____

_____

What is the New Testament canon?

_____

_____

_____

REMEMBER

The Bible is unique because although it is made up of 66 individual books and letters, it has complete unity and harmony. It is also unique because it has been supernaturally preserved.

To say the Bible is inspired means that it is "God breathed". That is, the words are from the mouth of God.

The New Testament canon is the list of books that passed the test for apostolic authorship, inspiration and authority and were included in the Bible.

The Bible is inerrant and infallible in all matters, including (but not limited to) faith, morals, the physical world, the universe, history, science and prophecy.

Seeking Son Light

Section 1

This Book We Call the Bible

Lesson 2

Why is the Bible Important?

The truth exists only in the
Word of God.

Section 1: This Book We Call The Bible
Lesson 2: Why Is The Bible Important?

Our need for the Bible is as great or greater now than at any other time in history. We are constantly bombarded with modern scientific discoveries and New Age thinking that challenge biblical truth. In fact, many today believe there is no absolute truth, morality is in the eye of the beholder and each of us is our own god.

Man's ideas come and go. They fall into and out of fashion, but the Bible has stood the test of time. How could anything less than absolute truth survive for over three thousand years? How can the concepts put forth in the Bible be as timely and pertinent today as when they were first written? Why have countless men and women been willing to die for the sake of the Bible?

People will not knowingly sacrifice themselves for the sake of a lie.

But what can the Bible teach a generation who already has access to information literally at the speed of light? If science unlocks a mystery of the universe in the morning, announcement of the discovery can circle the globe before dinner time. And not only is the release of information lightening fast, it is also accurate. It seems there are very few mysteries that science cannot reveal.

Or is that just another one of Satan's lies? (John 8:44) He would very much like for us to believe we have no need for the Bible. Satan wants us to worship science and technology, wants us to think we have the right to do exactly what we want to do with our bodies and he loves it when we actually believe that we are in control of our own destiny.

He confuses us with mental clutter, bombarding us with so much of it that we throw away old customs and establish new priorities that short-change God and His purpose for our life.

What kind of information does the Bible contain that causes Satan to work so hard to prevent us from seeing? For one thing, the Bible tells the truth about Satan himself and reveals that although he reigns on earth for a little while, he has a guaranteed reservation in the lake of fire whenever Jesus Christ decides to send him there (Revelation 20:10).

Let's explore the Bible and discover the truths revealed in it that are for our gain and Satan's loss.

The Bible Teaches Truth

One reason the Bible is so important today is that it teaches truth. We cannot recognize a lie if we don't know the truth.

The truth exists only in the Word of God. *(John 17:17)*

As we grow in our faith, we learn that if a fact is in the Bible, it is true. And as we learn more truth, the lies become easier to spot.

Some time ago, a "Magic Card Game" was circulating on the Internet. When the game opened, the screen displayed four cards: Queen of

Diamonds, Jack of Spades, Ten of Clubs and the Ace of Hearts. The player was instructed to concentrate on a single card. It could be any of the four cards but the player was to focus on that card and no other. He was told that if he concentrated hard enough, that very card would disappear!

The player was instructed to concentrate on his card for a sufficient amount of time, then go on to the next page and look for his card. Miraculously, the player's card is gone, apparently disappearing through his sheer mental capabilities.

That was the lie. The truth was that all four of the original cards were gone, having been replaced by the Queen of Clubs, Jack of Diamonds, Ten of Hearts and the Ace of Spades!

Once the truth is revealed, the lie can easily be seen for what it is.

The Bible Reveals our Purpose in Life

In 2002, the phenomenon known as "The Purpose Driven Life" hit bookstores across the nation and the rest, as they say, is history. The devotional and self-help book sold more than 30 million copies in its first five years in publication and was updated, revised and re-packaged for re-release on its tenth anniversary.

Author Rick Warren had hit a nerve. People are hungry to know why they are here: to discover their reason for being. With all due respect to the author, people do not need Mr. Warren to reveal the purpose of their lives.

Only God can reveal the purpose of our lives, and He has done so in the pages of the Bible. *(Ephesians 1:11)*

In the beginning, God created man to fellowship with Him and that is why man was created in God's image. He was to have dominion over all the earth, enjoy his work and glorify God in the process (Genesis 1:27-28). But when sin entered the world through Adam, the fellowship with God was broken, not only for Adam but for all of his descendants for all time. Work became difficult and fruitless and did not bring satisfaction as tending the Garden had done (Genesis 3:17-19).

Only through restoring our relationship with God through Jesus Christ can we begin to discover our purpose in this life. Our true purpose is to know God, to glorify Him and enjoy our relationship with Him forever (1 Thessalonians 4:7).

We come to know God through the Bible. We come to know His character and His divine attributes. And as we come to know Him, we discover our own purpose.

Solomon was the wisest and wealthiest man who ever lived (1 Kings 4:29-34; 2 Chronicles 9:13-14). There was nothing on earth that he could not have and his wealth and privilege separated him from God for a time. However, his book of Ecclesiastes opens with this statement:

"Meaningless! Meaningless!" says the Teacher. "Utterly meaningless!

Everything is meaningless!"

(Ecclesiastes 1:2, NIV)

These are not the words of a contented man. Solomon had come to realize that life apart from God was futile and not worth living (Ecclesiastes 12:13).

Many of us believe that if only we could win the lottery, we would finally find true happiness. Really? Human beings were created to fellowship with God, glorify Him and put Him first in our lives. Anything we allow to take God's place defeats that purpose.

Every good thing comes from God (James 1:17). How ironic that we struggle so hard to gather up all the good things in life, separating ourselves from God in the process, when He has already promised to give them to us as a gift (Matthew 7:11).

The Bible is Our Source of Peace

Only the Bible can provide us with peace and comfort in these turbulent times. God is not startled by the morning headlines. He is not thrown off balance by the lead story on the evening news. For those who do not follow God, thoughts of what the future holds can be terrifying.

But those who belong to Him are confident that all things will work for good and they are safe in His care. *(Romans 8:28)*

The Bible teaches us to live with an eternal perspective, something we cannot do without the truth of the Bible to back it up. We are taught that we do not belong to this world; we are foreigners here (Philippians 3:20). Although we have little or no control over what happens in this life, we can be absolutely assured as to what awaits us in the next: eternity with our loving Savior (John 3:14-16).

Some whose faith has not matured mistakenly believe that following Christ leads to a life of ease: no financial worries, perfectly behaved and successful children, and happy relationships. In fact, the Bible promises exactly the opposite. Jesus tells us that we will be persecuted and hated because of our love for Him (Matthew 10:22). Many Christians, even up to this present age, suffer terribly at the hands of those who love evil.

As we come to know the Apostles through the Bible, we see men who were undeniably worldly and undisciplined become humble yet fearless supporters of Christ. All but one became martyrs for their faith. What caused this change? They experienced a change in their perspective, preferring to store their treasures not on this earth but in Heaven (Matthew 6:20). They lived with an eternal perspective.

The Bible Reveals the Mysteries of the Past and the Future

The Bible reveals information that we could not otherwise know. It tells the true story of how we and the world we live in were created.

Of the approximately 2,500 prophecies contained in the Bible, about 2,000 have already been fulfilled. And they have been fulfilled to the letter. These are not prophecies of the type that today's so-called psychics or mediums foretell. They were revealed by God and we have every reason to believe that the prophecies remaining unfulfilled to date will eventually be fulfilled as completely and accurately as those that have already come to pass.

The Bible reveals that the earth hangs on nothing in space (Job 26:7). If the Bible had been written by mere mortals, how could they have known that? Even during the time of Columbus, many still believed the earth was a flat disk even though the Bible revealed the truth centuries before.

The Bible does not change. It is certain, true and accurate in all it says. In cases today where the Bible and science do not agree, it is simply because science has not caught up with what the Author of the Bible knows to be true. Christians must stand firm in their belief and faith in the Bible.

LESSON 2–SUMMARY

READ

John 8:44, Revelation 20:10, John 17:17, Ephesians 1:11, Genesis 1:27-28, Genesis 3:17-19, 1 Thessalonians 4:7, 1 Kings 4:29-34, 2 Chronicles 9:13-14, Ecclesiastes 1:2, Ecclesiastes 12:13, James 1:17, Matthew 7:11, Philippians 3:20, John 3:14-16, Matthew 10:22, Matthew 6:20, Job 26:7

REFLECT

Why is the Bible important today?

_____

_____

_____

How can we learn to live in peace in these turbulent times?

_____

_____

_____

Does the Bible teach that this life on earth will be easy if we only follow Christ?

_____

_____

_____

Why doesn't science always agree with the Bible?

_____

_____

_____

REMEMBER

We cannot recognize a lie if we don't know truth. The Bible teaches truth.

Life lived apart from God is futile and worthless. The treasures of this world cannot bring true happiness and peace.

Christians can live in peace in these turbulent times by having an eternal perspective. The Bible teaches Christians that they would be persecuted and hated in this world simply because they follow Christ, but by storing our treasures in Heaven, we can look forward to eternity with our Savior.

In cases where science disagrees with the Bible, it is because science has not yet caught up with what the Author of the Bible knows to be true.

Seeking Son Light

Section 1

This Book We Call the Bible

Lesson 3

Can We Trust the Bible? (Part 1)

We can have a high level of certainty that the Bible is a reliable and accurate document.

Section 1:   This Book We Call the Bible
Lesson 3:   Can We Trust the Bible? (Part 1)

When we consider whether the Bible is trustworthy, the issue is actually twofold:

- The trustworthiness of the biblical text.
- The trustworthiness of the biblical teachings.

This lesson will discuss the issue of the reliability of the biblical text. Part 2 of the lesson will address whether we can trust what the Bible teaches.

Textual Criticism is an area of study concerning the reliability of ancient texts. The term *Lower Criticism* refers to that portion of the study related to the identification and removal of transcription errors. *Higher Criticism* concerns itself with the issues of authorship and dating of the manuscripts.

The mission of textual critics is to study the copies of ancient literature in an attempt to reconstruct a manuscript that is as close as possible to the original.

Two important factors have an impact on the critics' work:

- The number of copies that are available for study.
- The amount of time that passed between the date of the original and the oldest available copy.

These are examples of some famous ancient literature:

- Caesar's *Gallic Wars* was written around 50 B.C. The oldest copies possessed today were made some 900 years later, and there are fewer than one dozen good manuscripts.
- The *History of Thucydides* was written around 400 B.C. and the earliest complete manuscript available today was made 1,300 years after it was written.
- There are only five or so copies of any writings of Aristotle (384-322 B.C.) and the earliest copy available today was made 1,400 years after the original.

This small number of copies available for study means that the critics have very limited resources for their work. And with the vast amount of time that passed between the writing of the original and the oldest known copy, there is a greater risk for undiscoverable error in transmission. Therefore historians debate the reliability of the copies that are possessed today of this literature.

So how does the Bible stack up against other ancient works?

As mentioned earlier, there is a direct link between the number of ancient manuscripts available for study and the ability of scholars to determine how close the text we have today is to the original manuscripts. There are more copies of biblical manuscripts and fragments of manuscripts than there are of any other ten pieces of ancient literature *combined*. One source estimates there are over 24,000 manuscripts and fragments of the New Testament text.

Our oldest complete manuscript of the New Testament was made a little more than 300 years after the original was written. Remember that the reliability of the text we have today is greater because a shorter amount of time passed between the date of the original and the date of the oldest available copy.

> The Bible far outweighs any other ancient book with regard to the number and quality of manuscript copies in existence today, and these facts allow us to have a high level of certainty that the Bible is a reliable and accurate document.

The Early Church Fathers

After the beginning of the second century A.D., other men stepped forward to spread the gospel and to ensure the purity of the teachings of the original Apostles, all of whom had died by this time. Among them were Polycarp, Irenaeus of Lyons, Clement of Rome and Eusebius, to name but a few. These men left numerous writings in which they quoted the letters and books that eventually became the New Testament.

> One scholar has determined that except for 11 verses, the entire New Testament can be reconstructed by using the writings of the early church fathers alone.

In these writings, there are more than 86,000 quotations attributed to the Apostles. This is a huge consideration in determining the accuracy and reliability of our modern texts. No other ancient literary work can make such a claim, and this is yet another reason to believe that the Holy Spirit was at work in the creation and preservation of God's Word.

Old Testament

The evidence discussed thus far has concerned only the New Testament. But is the Old Testament equally reliable?

The Hebrew Bible, better known to us as the Old Testament, was written over a period of 1,000 years, from 1400 B.C. to 400 B.C. At that time, writing was done on papyrus and on leather scrolls. The climate in Palestine was not conducive to the preservation of the papyrus, and leather scrolls were worn out. As a result, there is no remaining evidence outside the Bible itself to assist scholars in their analysis of the accuracy and reliability of the text.

The Scriptures were sacred to the Jews and they treated them with great reverence and respect. Because the Scriptures were written on perishable materials, it was frequently necessary for them to be recopied. Men who were specially trained in the precise and painstaking methods used in copying the Scriptures were referred to as *scribes*. For example, the scribes would count the number of verses in a book and mark the middle verse, verifying that the same verse was in the middle of the copy. In addition, they never worked from memory. They referred back to the original before writing each individual letter. If more than two corrections had to be made to the copy, the entire copy was destroyed. Such extreme measures helped to ensure that the Old Testament text we have today is accurate and reliable.

Prior to the discovery of the Dead Sea Scrolls in 1947, the oldest known Old Testament manuscript dated to about 1000 A.D. The Scrolls contain every book in the Old Testament except for the book of Esther. This single discovery resulted in Old Testament manuscripts dating back to the first century before Christ, and they bring us one thousand years closer to the originals.

The discovery of the Dead Sea Scrolls also allowed scholars to confirm the accuracy of the scribes who copied the text, and they found that the level of accuracy was astounding. In the entire book of Isaiah for example, only thirteen discrepancies were found and none of those discrepancies were related to faith and practice. The work of the Jewish scribes stood the test of time and has helped to ensure the accuracy of the biblical text we have today.

Dr. Clark Pinnock, Professor of Interpretation of McMasters University, in his book, "Set Forth Your Case", wrote an appropriate summary for this lesson:

"There exists no document from the ancient world witnessed by so excellent a set of textual and historical testimonies, and offering so superb an array of historical data on which an intelligent decision may be made. An honest man cannot dismiss a source of this kind. Skepticism regarding the historical credentials of Christianity is based upon an irrational bias."

LESSON 3 – SUMMARY

READ

Luke 1:1-4, Acts 1:1-2

REFLECT

What is textual criticism?

_____

_____

_____

What are two important factors that have an impact on textual critics' work?

_____

_____

_____

How do the writings of the early church fathers affect our study of the New Testament text today?

_____

_____

_____

REMEMBER

Textual Criticism is an area of study concerning the reliability of ancient texts, including the biblical texts.

Two important factors have an impact on the work of textual critics: (1) The number of copies available for study, and (2) the amount of time that passed between the original and the oldest available copy.

The large number of ancient New Testament manuscripts available for study helps scholars to have a high degree of confidence that the biblical text is accurate and very close to the original.

Except for 11 verses, the New Testament text can be completely reconstructed by using only the writings of the early church fathers who quoted the Apostles more than 86,000 times.

The discovery of the Dead Sea Scrolls was the most important event in the twentieth century in terms of biblical archaeology.

Seeking Son Light

Section 1
This Book We Call the Bible

Lesson 4
Can We Trust the Bible? (Part 2)

God's Word is alive. His words are
spirit and life.

Section 1: This Book We Call the Bible
Lesson 4: Can We Trust the Bible? (Part 2)

In the previous lesson, we discussed why we can be confident that the biblical texts are accurate, reliable and very close to the originals. It is important to have a high degree of confidence that the texts are accurate because we rely on the biblical teachings for nothing less than eternal salvation.

But while the accuracy of the text can be scientifically proven, how can we know that what the text says is true? Even though we feel confident that the text we have today says the same things as the original, how can we know that the teachings and stories were true even then?

Certainly faith plays an important role in our ability to believe and accept the Bible, but that does not mean logic should be thrown out the window.

> God created human beings to be intelligent creatures who possess the ability for critical thinking through logic and reasoning. *(Acts 19:8)*

Here are some of the reasons we can be confident in what the Bible teaches.

Jesus Believed It

The most compelling evidence that the Bible is trustworthy and is exactly what it says it is, is that Jesus believed it. He referred to "the Law and the

Prophets" (that's the Old Testament to us) many times during His ministry. Several references were made to the prophecies in the Scriptures and how He was the fulfillment of those prophecies (Luke 4:16-21). Jesus used Old Testament teachings to defeat Satan in the wilderness (Matthew 4:4-10) and spoke of Moses' foretelling of His coming (John 5:46-47). Finally, in the story of Lazarus and the rich man, Jesus tells that if a person did not believe the Scriptures, neither would he believe a person who returned from the dead (Luke 16: 31). Jesus *knew* that the Scriptures were true and His confirmation should be all the reason we need to accept them as such.

The Apostles Believed It

The men who lived with and learned from Jesus for three years believed in the accuracy of Scripture and believed it to be God's Word. Peter knew that his own death was imminent, and after the death of the other Apostles, believers would need continued encouragement and truth (2 Peter 1:12-15). In his last letter to Timothy, Paul also emphasized his belief in the Scriptures:

> "...all Scripture is given by inspiration of God, and is profitable for doctrine, for reproof, for correction, for instruction in righteousness." *(2 Timothy 3:16)*

There is no question that Jesus and the Apostles accepted the Scriptures as the true and trustworthy Word of God.

Fulfillment of Prophecy Confirms the Truth of the Bible

The Bible contains hundreds of prophecies, both in the Old and New Testaments. Many of these have already come to pass, such as the Jewish exile to Babylon (Leviticus 26:33-34), the conquest of Alexander the Great (Daniel 8:5-8), and the world-wide spread of the gospel (Acts 1:7-8; Mark 4:30-32). Others, such as the second coming of Christ, are yet to be fulfilled. However, the detail with which the prophecies were stated and the accuracy in their fulfillment is reason for us to believe that the prophecies which remain unfulfilled will eventually occur exactly as they are stated in Scripture.

Prophecy also speaks to the supernatural character of the Bible. The prophecies in the book of Daniel regarding the conquest of Alexander the Great are so detailed and accurate that for centuries, skeptics have insisted that the book was written after the events occurred. Accurately predicting future events is not a stretch for the omniscient God of the Universe.

The Bible Changes Lives

Dennis Selfridge of Harlowton Wesleyan Church says,

"God's Word is alive. His words are spirit and life. There is no other book that can make such a claim."

The Bible can and does change lives (Hebrews 4:12).

Sean Sellers, a professed Satanist, was not yet 18 years old when he killed a convenience store clerk ("just to see what it felt like to kill someone") and later, both of his parents as they slept. While awaiting execution for his crimes, Sellers was given a Bible in prison and converted to Christianity.

In 1983, Karla Faye Tucker killed two people with a pickaxe while under the influence of drugs and alcohol and was the first woman to be executed in Texas since 1863. As she sat on death row, she accepted a Bible from the prison ministry program and after reading it fell to her knees in her cell and asked God for forgiveness.

These are just two examples, albeit dramatic ones, of how God's Word changes lives. Humans are born in darkness and in their "natural" state are controlled by the prince of this world, Satan (John 3:19-20). Jesus said that Satan himself is a liar and is the father of all liars (John 8:44). Unfortunately, human beings who do not know truth, which is found only in the Bible, believe the lies and become liars themselves. God's Word sheds light on and reveals truth (John 3:21), and those who listen to and read the Bible come to realize that they have been following a liar. Through the work of the Holy Spirit, the lies are replaced with truth (1 Corinthians 2:14).

We have a choice about what we allow to take up space in our hearts and minds. If we choose poorly and allow lies and worldly desires to fill our minds and drive our actions, there is little room left for the Holy Spirit to do His work. And what is that work? The Holy Spirit works to conform us to the likeness of Christ. The more time we spend reading and studying the Bible, the more like Christ we become.

In order for a person's life to be changed by the Bible, that person must make a deliberate and conscious decision to accept the Bible as his or her ultimate authority.

The Bible is a road map that shows us how to reach our destination of living eternally with Christ. Without referring frequently to the map, we are prone to swerving off the road and failing to reach our destination at all. When we follow God's map and rules of the road, we have assurance of a safe arrival in Heaven (James 1:21-25).

LESSON 4 – SUMMARY

READ

Acts 19:8, Luke 4:16-21, Matthew 4:4-10, John 5:46-47, Luke 16: 31, 2 Peter 1:12-15, 2 Timothy 3:16, Leviticus 26:33-34, Daniel 8:5-8, Acts 1:7-8, Mark 4:30-32, Hebrews 4:12, John 3:19-20, John 8:44, John 3:21, 1 Corinthians 2:14, James 1:21-25

REFLECT

What are four reasons we know we can trust the teachings in the Bible?

_____

_____

_____

How does fulfilled prophecy reflect on those prophecies that remain unfulfilled today?

_____

_____

_____

How does the Bible change lives?

_____

_____

_____

What must a person do in order for his life to be changed by the Bible?

_____

_____

_____

REMEMBER

We can have confidence that the biblical teachings are true because Jesus believed them, the Apostles believed them, prophecy confirms them and we can see lives changed because of the Bible.

Because prophecy was fulfilled exactly as it was written in the Bible, we have every reason to expect unfulfilled prophecy to eventually come to pass exactly as described in Scripture.

The Bible changes lives by shedding light on and revealing truth, and by exposing lies for what they are.

The first step in achieving a changed life through the Bible is to make the deliberate and conscious decision to accept the Bible as one's ultimate authority.

Seeking Son Light

Section 1
This Book We Call the Bible

Lesson 5
Who Wrote the Bible?

God decided *what* needed to be said
and the human writers decided *how* to
say it.

Section 1: This Book We Call the Bible
Lesson 5: Who Wrote the Bible?

The Bible is referred to as a "book" but because it is made up of many individual books and letters, the term "library" could also apply.

When we enter a library, we see volumes written by many different authors. Some authors have written more than one book. The writings cover a variety of topics including history, current events, adventure, romance, poetry and futuristic thrillers. They include law books and "how to" books.

The authors' styles are as varied as the topics. Some write in a very straight-forward, easy to understand manner and others are more dramatic and draw us into the story with vivid descriptions and colorful language.

Now, we know that God is the true author of the Bible but He used human writers to record His message. These writers put God's message in their own words but the Holy Spirit's superintending of the work ensured the accuracy and infallibility of the Scriptures (2 Peter 1:20-21).

Old Testament

The Jewish historian Josephus wrote his autobiography in about A.D. 90, and in it, he recounts the story of how Emperor Titus gave him the sacred scrolls from the temple in Jerusalem when the temple and the city itself were destroyed by the Romans in A.D. 70. These scrolls were sacred to the Jews because they were written by the prophets, from Moses to Malachi.

Josephus wrote, "We have...only twenty-two books which contain the records of all the past times, which are justly believed to be divine." He goes on to identify the writings: "Five belong to Moses;...the prophets who were after Moses wrote down what was done in their times in thirteen books;...the remaining four books contain hymns to God and precepts for the conduct of human life."

These books listed by Josephus in A.D. 90 are the same, and only, books that are included in our Old Testament today. So how is it that Josephus named twenty-two scrolls and yet our Old Testament includes 39 books? It is simply because some scrolls were separated into multiple books when the text was translated from the original language.

Unless the author is identified in the text itself, as in the book of Daniel (Daniel 12:5), we cannot know with complete certainty who actually wrote the various portions of the Old Testament, although Bible scholars do have solid evidence that supports their theories concerning authorship of the books. We must not forget, however, that God is behind every word in Scripture.

God decided *what* needed to be said and the human writers decided *how* to say it.

Shown below is a very brief summary of the generally accepted authors of the Old Testament books. For greater detail, refer to a Bible with good study notes concerning authorship and dates of the books.

- Moses is credited with writing the first five books of the Old Testament (Numbers 12:6-8): Genesis, Exodus, Leviticus, Numbers and Deuteronomy.
- Samuel is most likely the author of several books, including Judges, Ruth and 1 and 2 Samuel. He also probably contributed to the books of 1 and 2 Kings and 1 and 2 Chronicles.
- Ezra wrote Ezra and Nehemiah as a single book. They were separated into two individual books when they were translated from the original language.
- David, Asaph, Moses and probably others contributed to the book of Psalms.
- Solomon wrote three books: Proverbs, Ecclesiastes and Song of Songs, sometimes called Song of Solomon.
- Jeremiah wrote Jeremiah and Lamentations.
- Mordecai is generally considered to be the author of the book of Esther.
- Joshua is credited with writing the book of Joshua (Joshua 24:26).
- The remaining books, except for Job, were most likely written by the prophets whose names they bear. Authorship for the book of Job is unknown.

Why did the authors fail to identify themselves in their works? It is because they were writing to glorify God, not themselves. Remember that it is the message that is important, not the messenger (Romans 1:2; Hebrews 1:1).

New Testament

There are twenty-seven books in the New Testament. Of these, no fewer than twenty-one were written by the Apostles themselves. The remaining books were written either by other eye-witnesses or from eye-witness accounts.

While Mark was not an apostle, the Apostle Peter was his source of information. Mark may have been one of the many disciples who followed Jesus and some have even speculated that the young man whose garment was seized when Jesus was arrested was Mark himself (Mark 14:51-52).

James (not the Apostle James) and Jude were not only eye-witnesses but as Jesus' half-brothers, they had special insight into His human and yet divine nature. It is interesting to keep this in mind when studying the books that bear their names.

The gospel of Luke and the book of Acts were written by Luke, a medical doctor and historian who had close ties to Paul (2 Timothy 4:11). Although there is no evidence that Luke was an eye-witness to the events surrounding Jesus' ministry, information from the Apostle Paul undoubtedly contributed a great deal to these two books.

Authorship of the book of Hebrews is uncertain. Although possibly written by Paul, the writing style differs so significantly from his known works that some scholars feel certain he was not the author of Hebrews. In any case, it was obviously written by someone with a deep understanding of the theological truths.

Paul made the single largest contribution to the composition of the New Testament, having written thirteen books, and possibly fourteen depending on how one counts Hebrews. The remaining books in the New Testament were written by the Apostles whose names appear in the book titles:

- Matthew
- John (the Gospel of John; 1, 2 and 3 John; Revelation)
- Peter (1 and 2 Peter)

Any serious study of the writers of the Bible will result in amazement that so many people from such varied backgrounds and occupations could all contribute to a book that has such unity and cohesiveness as the Bible. It again speaks to the divine origin and supernatural elements in the Bible.

LESSON 5–SUMMARY

READ

2 Peter 1:20-21, Daniel 12:5, Numbers 12:6-8, Joshua 24:26, Romans 1:2, Hebrews 1:1, Mark 14:51-52, 2 Timothy 4:11

REFLECT

Why can the Bible be referred to as a library?

_____

_____

_____

What is significant about the list of "sacred scrolls" identified by Josephus in A.D. 90?

_____

_____

_____

Why can we have confidence in the New Testament books that were not written by the Apostles?

_____

_____

_____

Why is it important that the Bible was written by nearly 40 different people and yet it has unity and cohesiveness?

_____

_____

_____

REMEMBER

Because the Bible is made up of many different books written by many different people, it can be referred to as a library.

The list of twenty-two "sacred scrolls" identified by Josephus is significant because it is the oldest complete list of the books which make up the Old Testament we have today.

The contents of the twenty-two scrolls were separated into 39 different books when they were translated from the original language.

We can have confidence in all of the New Testament books because they were either written by eye-witnesses or from eye-witness accounts.

The Bible has unity and cohesiveness because its creation was superintended by the Holy Spirit, even though nearly 40 different people participated in its writing.

Seeking Son Light

Section 1
This Book We Call the Bible

Lesson 6
How Should We Study the Bible? (Part 1)

It is the Holy Spirit who enables us to
understand God's Word.

Section 1: This Book We Call the Bible
Lesson 6: How Should We Study the Bible? (Part 1)

There are literally hundreds of books on the market today that teach various methods for Bible study, and there are about as many different authors as there are methods. Some methods suggest using a Bible that does not contain paragraph or chapter divisions because this allows the student to determine the boundaries of particular passages being studied. Some methods suggest the use of commentaries while others say that a commentary is someone else's interpretation and that it takes away from the student the joy of discovering biblical truth for himself.

Some methods are too basic and will not be challenging enough while others are way too complex for a beginner.

The suggestions and guidelines contained in these lessons are very basic and are at the introductory level. They are intended for the person who is new to Bible study and who has little or no experience with the Bible at all. It emphasizes that the most important method of all is to simply spend time with the Bible on a regular basis (Matthew 4:4).

The use of study aids, including commentaries, is encouraged. Commentaries created by righteous men who have a talent for writing and who possess spiritual gifts for teaching and exhortation are excellent tools for a new Bible student. They help explain the Scripture itself and provide cultural information that may affect the interpretation of a certain passage. However, care must be taken in the selection of suitable material and this is discussed in more detail later.

Remember that it is the Holy Spirit who enables us to understand God's Word. *(1 Corinthians 2:14)*

He progressively reveals the truth to us. The reader will experience the joy of discovering wisdom that is only revealed to those with a pure heart and love for God's Word.

Choose a Bible

The most important thing to bring to Bible study is the Bible itself! Going to a Christian bookstore and buying a Bible sounds easy enough but a new student can be overwhelmed by the choices:

Choose a translation: KJV, NKJV, NIV, NASB, RSV, TNIV, NLT. What!?

Choose a study type: Life Application, Women's Study Bible, Teen Adventure Study Bible, Inductive Study Bible, Parallel Bible, Chronological Bible, Archaeological Bible, Apologetics Bible. Are you kidding?

Choose a binding: Hardbound, paperback, vinyl, fabric, bonded leather, genuine leather. Do you want that with tabs or without? Oh my!

Relax! Choosing a Bible is not as daunting a task as it might seem at first. But it is important to choose wisely and the reasons why are discussed below.

Translations: The task facing Bible translators is difficult and extremely important. Not only are they converting a manuscript written in an ancient foreign language into modern-day English, but they must do so in a way that is reader-friendly and yet does not compromise the integrity of the original message.

The King James Version (KJV) was completed in 1611 and is still considered by some today to be the only acceptable Bible translation. It is difficult to read due to its outdated language but the scholars involved in the work were faithful and conscientious. The New King James Version (NKJV) is a revision of the original but uses the vocabulary and language structure used by people today, making it much more reader-friendly than the 1611 version.

A newer translation is the New American Standard Bible (NASB) and it receives high marks for accuracy and faithfulness to the original text, although some believe it is not written in the smoothest modern English. This is a good choice for the serious Bible student.

The New International Version (NIV) is one of the most popular translations today. It was completed by a large group of competent scholars and is written in a smooth and reader-friendly manner. However, it is a "sentence equivalent" rather than a "word-for-word" translation, and some today feel this dilutes the original message.

The New Living Translation (NLT) is probably the most reader-friendly version, but it is yet another step away from the purity of the original manuscripts. It is a "thought-for-thought" translation which means that the reader is receiving the interpretation of the translator. This is probably not the best choice for serious study.

Study Type: For lack of a better term, "study type" is used in this lesson to refer to the multitude of study Bibles available today. Popular study types include the Life Application Study Bible, the Women of Faith Study Bible, the Archaeological Study Bible and the Apologetics Study Bible.

It is most important to understand that the Bible's study type does not affect the biblical text itself. The study type refers only to the study notes in the Bible.

The notes and articles in a particular study Bible are designed to explain and apply Scripture from a specific point of view. For example, notes in the Women of Faith Study Bible are written to provide insight regarding the application of Scripture specifically to women; the notes in the Archaeological Study Bible place emphasis on biblical archaeology. The biblical text itself in the NIV translation is identical in both the Women of Faith Study Bible and the Archaeological Study Bible.

Binding: The only recommendation concerning the binding is to select a cover that is durable. And regarding the color of your Bible, remember: It doesn't matter what color your Bible is as long as it is "read"! (John 17:17)

To summarize: The New International Version provides an excellent balance between loyalty to the message in the original languages and consideration of the twenty-first century reader. Cross-reference indexing in the margins is a must and thumb tabs are helpful in navigating through the Scripture. A Bible with a durable cover should be chosen, and the print size should be considered as well. A Bible will be your close companion for many years to come (Ezra 7:10).

Other Study Aids

The serious student will want to obtain certain other study aids. A concordance is an alphabetical index of the principle words used in the Bible. This is especially helpful when doing a topical study. A Bible dictionary is a cross between an English dictionary and an encyclopedia. It defines terms and provides background information for many topics related to Bible study. Commentaries are a valuable resource and help a new Bible student better understand the Scripture. One might even wish to use two separate commentaries in order to get a broader view and better insight into the Scripture being studied.

Do not ignore this word of caution. A bookstore, even a Christian bookstore, is like a smorgasbord: Everything looks wonderful but not everything is good for you. Books touting liberal ideas may be thought provoking and challenging but they have no place in the library of the new Bible student or the immature Christian (2 Timothy 2:15). Instead choose books by well known and respected authors and publishers. For example, commentaries by Warren Weirsby, J. Vernon McGee and John MacArthur are all based on biblical truth and are reliable resources.

LESSON 6–SUMMARY

READ

Matthew 4:4, 1 Corinthians 2:14, John 17:17, Ezra 7:10, 2 Timothy 2:15

REFLECT

Why must one take care in selecting a Bible study method?

_____

_____

_____

What role does the Holy Spirit have in our Bible study?

_____

_____

_____

What is the difference between a Bible translation and a Bible's study type?

_____

_____

_____

Why does a new Bible student need to be careful in buying study aids, even at a Christian bookstore?

_____

_____

_____

REMEMBER

A new student should select a Bible study method that is challenging and yet not too advanced. A student will know when he is ready to "graduate" to a more advance method.

Without the work of the Holy Spirit, we would be unable to understand the Scriptures.

The biblical text in a particular translation (KJV, NIV, NASB, etc.) is the same regardless of what the study type is (for example: Women of Faith Study Bible, Life Application Study Bible, etc.)

Just because a book is sold at a Christian bookstore does not guarantee that it contains sound doctrine and is valuable for Bible study.

Seeking Son Light

Section 1

This Book We Call the Bible

Lesson 7

How Should we Study the Bible? (Part 2)

The ultimate goal of Bible study is to apply its teachings to your life.

Section 1:   This Book We Call the Bible
Lesson 7:   How Should We Study the Bible? (Part 2)

The previous lessons discussed what the Bible is, why it is important, how we know it is trustworthy and who participated in writing it. Now you are ready to pick up the Bible and actually begin reading, studying and discovering for yourself how this Book can impact your life.

There is effort involved in developing the habit of daily Bible reading. One should designate a specific place and time for reading. Choose a quiet, comfortable place where interruption and distraction will be minimized. Many people find early morning to be the optimal time for reading while others prefer to end their day with the Bible.

No one can deny there is a difference between simply reading the Bible, referred to in this lesson as devotional reading, and serious Bible study. Devotional reading should be done with a quiet spirit. That is, put the world and its cares aside while you spend time in the Bible. The challenges and obstacles of everyday life will still be there waiting for you after you finish your devotional time (Matthew 6:34). Read carefully and consider what you are reading (Joshua 1:8). In your Bible, underline words and phrases that you find particularly touching or thought provoking and go back periodically to review them.

When studying the Bible, remember that quality is more important than quantity. It is better to give a small

passage in-depth consideration than to quickly peruse a larger section of Scripture without giving it the full attention it deserves.

There is no substitute for quality time spent reading the Bible. Scholars recommend reading the same book two or three times until its message becomes familiar and understandable. New truths will be discovered with every reading (Romans 10:17). This creates the foundation for a lifetime of learning truth and living truth.

The natural progression from devotional reading is more serious Bible study. Like anything else, a greater effort yields greater results. There are literally no limits to the depth to which the Scriptures can be studied.

It is important to remember that the ultimate goal of Bible study is to apply its teachings to your life *(James 1:22)*. It is possible to *academically* learn biblical truth without allowing it to be absorbed into your heart and result in a changed life.

God intends for both our minds and our hearts to benefit from His Word.

When a serious Bible study is undertaken, one of two approaches is generally used. These are (1) topical study and (2) book-by-book study.

Both of these approaches are good and can be used in conjunction with one another.

In a topical study, a specific topic is studied in great detail. The topic could be, for example, a person, a doctrine, or a certain geographical location. A topical index such as Nave's Topical Index is invaluable for conducting this type of study.

In a book-by-book study, a specific Bible book is analyzed and typically includes a verse-by-verse study. This is a huge undertaking for a beginner but the use of one or more commentaries will help keep the student on track and provide background information that will certainly enhance the results of the study.

At the beginning of a book-by-book study, determine the identity of the author, the original audience and the approximate date the book was written. What were the circumstances of the author and/or the audience at that time? Most study Bibles will provide this information at the beginning of each book.

Read the book through once or twice without any study aids. After reading, see if you can answer these questions:

- *What was the overall theme or primary subject of the book?*
- *Did the book teach a lesson, and if so, what was it?*
- *What was the message the author was trying to convey to his original audience?*
- *What application, if any, does that message have for us today?*
- *Does the book provide an example for us to follow or an error for us to avoid?*

If these questions cannot be answered, read the book again.

After achieving a level of comfort with the book, go through it again, and this time, use study aids, such as one or more commentaries. Read the passage in the Bible, and then read the commentaries for that passage. Does the interpretation in the commentary differ from your own interpretation? If you are using more than one commentary, do those interpretations agree with one another?

Using two commentaries for studying the same Bible book is often enlightening. One would hope that the authors would be in complete agreement about the interpretation of specific passages, but that is not always the case.

Identifying the areas of disagreement gives the student the opportunity to delve more deeply into the Scriptures to determine his own conclusion.

Remaining within the guidelines provided by the commentaries prevents the student from going way off track in his investigation.

At this point, it is appropriate to repeat an earlier warning. Use care when selecting commentaries and other Bible study books. Steer away from the more liberal authors and stick with the more conservative orthodox teachers. Criteria for selecting biblically sound study material must include more than recognizing an author's name from the Best Seller list. Seek the counsel of a trusted pastor, elder or teacher when selecting study material.

Regardless of the method or approach that is used in Bible study, certain rules always apply:

- *Begin with prayer.* The Holy Spirit is our true guide in taking us through the Bible. Without the work of the Holy Spirit, we would remain hopelessly lost in the pages of Scripture, reading but not understanding, and unable to apply the teachings to our lives (1 Corinthians 1:18).
- *Let the Scriptures speak for themselves.* Do not go into the Bible with a preconceived idea of what it says and do not try to shape the Scriptures to make them fit your understanding. Go to it with an open mind and a prepared heart.
- *Read the Bible as you would any other literature.* The sentences are plainly stating exactly what they mean. That is, the Bible is meant to be taken literally. Many people try to allegorize Scripture, believing that the message is hidden and that it speaks only symbolically.

Remember that this is God's final message to us. Everything contained within its pages is meant to teach and inspire us. It is meant to warn us against the traps that ensnare so many, preventing them from finding truth. Why then would God write it so it could not be understood?

- *Spend time with the Bible every day.* Even a few minutes alone with the Bible will bring great rewards.

LESSON 7 – SUMMARY

READ

Matthew 6:34, Joshua 1:8, Romans 10:17, James 1:22, 1 Corinthians 1:18

REFLECT

How can we prepare ourselves for devotional reading of the Bible?

_____

_____

_____

What is the best method for serious Bible study?

_____

_____

_____

What can we learn by referring to two separate commentaries for Bible study?

_____

_____

_____

Why can we be confident that the Bible was meant to be taken literally?

_____

_____

_____

REMEMBER

We should come to the Bible with a quiet spirit for devotional reading and clear our minds of worldly worries.

There is no "best" way to approach Bible study, except to be consistent and thorough.

It is interesting to utilize more than one commentary for Bible study in order to identify any differences in the interpretation of the same passage. This gives us the opportunity to study the passage more deeply and determine our own interpretation.

We know that the Bible is meant to be understood literally because it represents God's final message to us concerning righteous living. He wants us to read and completely understand the Bible's teachings in order to live a life that is pleasing to Him.

Seeking Son Light

Section 1

This Book We Call the Bible

Lesson 8

Answering Bible Critics

Some questions and difficulties are
to be expected from an ancient book
like the Bible whose historic settings
cover a period from the Bronze Age to
Roman times.

Section 1:   This Book We Call the Bible
Lesson 8:   Answering Bible Critics

As we share our faith with others, we will encounter those who are critical of Christianity in general and the Bible in particular. They believe the Bible represents the writings of primitive people who mistook certain events as miracles that in modern times can be explained in scientific terms.

The Bible describes many miracles. The Red Sea parted (Exodus 14:21-22), storms were calmed (Mark 4:39), sight was given to the blind (John 9:1-7), men walked on water (Matthew 14:25-27) and thousands were fed with a couple of fish and a few loaves of bread (Luke 9:13-17).

One thing these events have in common is that they cannot be accomplished by mere men operating within the laws of nature.

While the people who lived during those times did not have the scientific data we possess today, they did know that it was not normal for the sea to part and expose dry land. They knew that storms raged and could not be calmed with a simple word. And they were well aware that a couple of fish and a few loaves of bread would not feed thousands of people.

The ancients were not rocket scientists but they knew it was not normal for a man to walk on water!

What is a miracle? A *miracle* is (1) an extraordinary event manifesting divine intervention in human affairs, or (2) an extremely outstanding or unusual event, thing or accomplishment.

The events described above and others like them were due to the intrusion of a supernatural power into the natural world. There is no other explanation. The laws of nature can only be broken by the One who created them. The God who spoke the universe into existence chose to perform these miracles as proof that He was at work since the events could not have happened naturally.

If a person is determined not to believe that the Bible is true, there is nothing we can do to change him. Only the Holy Spirit has the power to work in that person's life and create a change of heart. We must remember that the Bible is about spiritual matters which cannot be understood by an unredeemed person. Spiritual things must be spiritually discerned. An understanding of Scripture is impossible outside the work of the Holy Spirit (1 Corinthians 2:14-15). As believers we should present our defense and pray that the veil will be lifted from the eyes of those who cannot see.

While some simply will not accept the Bible as truth, others may have genuine concerns and legitimate questions that can be resolved by a person who is prepared to defend God's Word.

Some questions and difficulties are to be expected from an ancient book like the Bible whose historic settings cover a period from the Bronze Age to Roman times.

What about contradictions? As students of the Bible, we are taught that the Bible contains no contradictions whatsoever. And yet there seems to be an abundance of them. For example:

- One book tells us that Judas threw the thirty pieces of silver into the Temple and then went out and hanged himself (Matthew 27:3-5). In another book, Judas used the money to purchase a field, and "there he fell head long, his body burst open and all his intestines spilled out." (Acts 1:18)
- One account describes two blind men sitting by the wayside (Matthew 9:27), and another mentions only "a certain blind man." (Luke 18:35)

Do these alleged contradictions mean that the Bible is unreliable? Absolutely not! These are possible explanations:

- Perhaps the money Judas threw into the Temple was used to purchase the field in which his body was found. Although he hanged himself, the limb or rope may have broken, causing his body to fall. Left undiscovered for some period of time, the body would bloat and eventually burst. Regarding the blind man receiving sight, is it not possible that Jesus gave sight to more than just one blind man? It is not inconceivable that the accounts describe different events.

An account will differ based on the writer's perspective and on his relationship to his intended audience. Matthew wrote his gospel primarily for the Jews. It is very likely that he would include details that were significant from a Jewish perspective which might be omitted from an account written for a non-Jewish audience.

Consider this. Three people were walking together when suddenly a red car and a blue car collided on the road in front of them. A green car turning onto the road from a side street swerved to avoid the accident and the car finally came to rest in someone's front yard. When the police arrived, they asked each of the witnesses to write down what they saw. One witness said the red car crossed the center line; another said the blue car was stopped on the street before the collision. The third witness said the green car caused the whole thing! The observations of each witness were based on their own perspectives and even though their accounts were different from one another, they all described the same event.

A true skeptic will not change his opinion, even when provided with sound and reasonable arguments in favor of the divine origin of the Bible. A Christian must make a deliberate choice to accept the Bible as his ultimate authority. For unredeemed souls, the prospect of submitting to the authority of another, even to God Himself, is quite distasteful. They justify their denial of Scripture by over-emphasizing biblical difficulties, such as alleged contradictions, without honestly trying to resolve the discrepancies and considering logical explanations.

In the end, the unsaved are buying into Satan's lie concerning the divinity and sovereignty of God (Romans 1:25). The contents of the Bible are absolutely priceless, worth more than silver and gold. We should consider it to be our most precious possession, not to be put on display and collect dust on a shelf, but to be devoured as heavenly food to nourish our souls.

LESSON 8 – SUMMARY

READ

Exodus 14:21-22, Mark 4:39, John 9:1-7, Matthew 14:25-27, Luke 9:13-17, 1 Corinthians 2:14-15, Matthew 27:3-5, Acts 1:18, Matthew 9:27, Luke 18:35, Romans 1:25

REFLECT

What do all Bible miracles have in common?

_____

_____

_____

Why might the telling of the same event contain discrepancies among the various Bible books?

_____

_____

_____

What should our response be to a person who is determined not to believe in the Bible?

_____

_____

_____

REMEMBER

All Bible miracles are events that cannot be accomplished by mere men operating within the laws of nature.

Each witness to an event sees it and describes it from his own perspective.

Christians should be prepared to defend the Bible to skeptics, but only the Holy Spirit can change the condition of a person's heart.

Seeking Son Light

Section 1

This Book We Call the Bible

For further reading…

"Exploring the Basics of the Bible" by R. Laird Harris

"How We Got Our Bible" by Charles C. Ryrie

"Know What You Believe" by Paul E. Little

"Know Why You Believe" by Paul E. Little

"Evidence that Demands a Verdict" by Josh McDowell

"Why We Believe the Bible" by Dr. Jim Denison

"Scriptures to Live By" by John MacArthur

"Be" Book Bible Commentaries by Warren Weirsby

"Through the Bible" by J. Vernon McGee

Seeking Son Light

Section 2
The Ten Commandments

Lesson 1
Laying Down the Law

God gave the Law to the people to
reveal their sin.

Section 2:   The Ten Commandments
Lesson 1:   Laying Down the Law

Less than three months after Moses left Egypt to lead the Israelites to the land of Canaan, God summoned him to the top of Mount Sinai to lay down the law.

At the mention of 'The Ten Commandments' many Americans today might first think of the epic 1956 movie with that title. We visualize the strong and handsome Charlton Heston trudging to the top of Mount Sinai as the smoke covered mountain trembled beneath the awesome power of God. Left to their own devices while Moses is away, the Israelites soon get into mischief by throwing a drunken orgy complete with human sacrifice, false idols and debauchery.

Reality for Moses was quite different than the way Charlton Heston portrayed him. Far from being the strong and confident leader we see in the movie, Moses begged God to send someone else to do the job (Exodus 4:13). He looked more like a shepherd than a Hollywood leading man and he had a speech impediment (Exodus 4:10)! However in spite of his shortcomings, or perhaps because of them, God used Moses as His liaison to communicate His laws and commandments to Israel.

The giving of the Law to the nation of Israel was one of the most dramatic events in human history. For forty days Moses met God face to face (Exodus 33:11) as He laid out the laws for His people. These included moral, ceremonial and civil laws which are collectively known as the "Mosaic Law" and which consist of 613 individual commandments. When

Moses returned to the people and told them what God had commanded, they said, "All that the LORD has spoken, we will do!" (Exodus 19:8).

The moral laws included the Ten Commandments:

1. You shall have no other gods before Me.
2. You shall not make for yourself an idol.
3. Do not disrespect the name of your God.
4. Remember the Sabbath and keep it holy.
5. Honor your father and mother.
6. Do not murder.
7. Do not commit adultery.
8. Do not steal.
9. Do not lie.
10. Do not covet anything that belongs to your neighbor.

We know that one reason God gave these laws to the nation of Israel was to set them apart from the pagans who lived in the land they were preparing to take. Through the centuries, the Jews knew they were the special people of God because they alone had received the Law. Eventually however we see that the Jews valued *having* the Law much more than they valued actually *keeping* it (Psalm 78:8-10). While they performed their duties as prescribed by the Law, their worship was nothing more than simply going through the motions and it was hollow and worthless to God.

Was God surprised that the Jews did not keep the Law? No. In fact, it was part of His original plan.

The main reason God gave the Law to Israel was to prove to them that they could not keep it.

What?

In its entirety, the Mosaic Law laid out the rules for perfect and righteous human conduct for their interaction with God and with one another. Of course, by nature, humans are neither perfect nor righteous. While the people had good intentions about keeping the Law ("All the LORD has spoken, we will do!") they did not realize how far they were from God's standard of righteousness. God knew they could not do everything He required of them but the people had not yet reached that conclusion (Romans 9:30-32).

God gave the Law to the people to reveal their sin.

And He left little room for error. He said, "Whoever keeps the whole law and yet stumbles at just one point is guilty of breaking all of it." (James 2:10)

Remember: Never was the purpose of the Law to remove sin. Its purpose was to reveal sin (Romans 7:7).

The purpose of the Law was to reveal our need for a Savior; that is, a perfect person who was capable of keeping all

of the Law and who would share His righteousness with all who asked.

In all of human history ... past, present and future ... only one person could do that job:

Jesus Christ

Large portions of the Mosaic Law included regulations for dealing with stolen livestock (Exodus 22:1), skin infections (Leviticus 13:2), foreign gods (Joshua 24:23) and treatment of slaves (Leviticus 25:44). We obviously know that today, we no longer need religious laws to govern issues like skin infections, foreign gods and treatment of slaves, and any problems regarding stolen livestock are governed by our civil laws. We have no obligation to the Mosaic Law concerning these issues. But what about moral issues? What about the Ten Commandments?

The New Testament writers tell us in no uncertain terms that Christians are under no obligation to keep any portion of the Mosaic Law (Galatians 5:18). That includes the Ten Commandments. But does that mean as Christians we are free to murder, lie, commit adultery and worship idols? As Paul says in his letter to the Romans, "Shall we sin because we are not under the law but under grace? May it never be!" (Romans 6:15)

Are the Ten Commandments in a class by themselves? Nearly every culture, society and religion has a set of moral and ethical standards that are similar to the Ten Commandments. This is because God has made Himself known to all men (Romans 1:18-20). We are told in Romans that although the Gentiles did not have the Law, they showed that the requirements of the Law were written on their hearts and their consciences also bore witness. (Romans 2:14-15)

God's moral code existed long before the Ten Commandments were written in stone. When Cain murdered Abel (Genesis 4:9-13) it was no less an abomination simply because he had not read that committing murder was a sin. Shem and Japheth understood the unwritten commandment to honor their father Noah even though Ham had disrespected him (Genesis 9:21-23). Joseph knew that having sex with Potiphar's wife was wrong (Genesis 39:6-10) even though God had not yet commanded the Israelites, "Do not commit adultery."

Christians receive salvation by grace alone. It is a gift from God that cannot be earned or achieved in any way other than belief and faith in Jesus Christ (Ephesians 2:8). Acceptance of Christ is the first step in our regeneration, our becoming new creatures. God's grace trains us to reject godless ways and worldly desires and to live self-controlled, upright and godly lives in the present age. *(J. Hampton Keithly: "The Mosaic Law: Its Function and Purpose in the New Testament")*

"Teacher, which is the greatest commandment in the Law?" In response to that question, Jesus said, "Love your God with all your heart and with all your soul and with all your mind. That is the first and greatest commandment. And the second is like it: Love your neighbor as yourself. All the Law and the Prophets hang on these two commandments." (Matthew 22:35-40) Jesus affirmed all Ten Commandments in His response:

- The first four commandments concern our relationship with God *(we are to love God with our entire being)*

- The last six commandments concern our relationship with one another *(love your neighbor as yourself)*

In the remaining lessons in this section, each of the Ten Commandments will be studied to discover what they meant for the people to whom they were originally given. We will also try to determine what application if any, the Ten Commandments have for Christians today.

LESSON 1–SUMMARY

READ

Exodus 4:13, Exodus 4:10, Exodus 33:11, Exodus 19:8, Psalm 78:8-10, Romans 9:30-32, James 2:10, Romans 7:7, Exodus 22:1, Leviticus 13:2, Joshua 24:23, Leviticus 25:44, Galatians 5:18, Romans 6:15, Romans 1:18-20, Romans 2:14-15, Genesis 4:9-13, Genesis 9:21-23, Genesis 39:6-10, Ephesians 2:8, Matthew 22:35-40

REFLECT

Why did God give the Laws to the nation of Israel?

_____

_____

_____

Why do so many cultures, societies and religions have a set of moral and ethical standards that are so similar to the Ten Commandments?

_____

_____

_____

What responsibility, if any, do Christians have today to live by the Ten Commandments?

_____

_____

_____

REMEMBER

God gave the Law to Israel to not only make them different from the pagans who lived in the land, but to prove to them that they could not keep the Law. The Law was designed to *reveal* sin.

Nearly every culture, society and religion has a set of moral and ethical standards that are similar to the Ten Commandments because God made Himself known to all men.

A Christian has no obligation to keep the Ten Commandments to achieve salvation, but Jesus reaffirmed the Ten Commandments in His teaching. A Christian will keep the commandments to show his love for Christ.

Seeking Son Light

Section 2

The Ten Commandments

Lesson 2

A Jealous God

"You shall have no other gods
before Me."

Section 2: The Ten Commandments
Lesson 2: A Jealous God

Commandment #1: You shall have no other gods before Me.

Commandment #2: You shall not worship false idols.

When Abraham Lincoln signed the Emancipation Proclamation on January 1, 1863, what would have happened if he had also proclaimed that all of the freed slaves were to be put onto ships and returned to Africa? Twelve generations had passed since Africans began to enter this country as slaves and virtually none of the approximately 500,000 slaves living in the United States at that time had ever been to Africa. They certainly wanted freedom from slavery but they also wanted to remain in the country of their birth: America.

The same was true of the Hebrew people living in Egypt. They desperately wanted freedom from slavery but 400 years had passed since their forefathers fled the famine in Canaan (Genesis 46:26-27). All of the Hebrews living at the time of the Exodus had been born in Egypt; it was the only home they had ever known. So while they cried out to God asking to be freed from their bondage, they might not have realized that leaving Egypt would also be part of the bargain.

We Have a God?

What did the Hebrews actually know about God? The Bible tells us that the Hebrew midwives knew and feared God (Exodus 1:15-17) so it is evident that the Hebrew people at least knew of His existence. They had no written Scriptures and whatever they did know about Him had been handed down orally. They most likely knew of the promises God had made to their forefathers, but after generations of mistreatment at the hands of the Egyptians, they quite possibly had a poor opinion of Him, thinking that any god who would leave his people stranded in a foreign land in slavery wasn't much of a god anyway.

So while they knew *of* God, they didn't really *know* God.

> ## God spoke further to Moses, "I am the LORD; and I appeared to Abraham, to Isaac and to Jacob as God Almighty, but by my name, LORD, I did not make myself known to them" *(Exodus 6:2-3)*

The Israelites, as they were called, were about to be introduced to Yahweh, the one true God and Creator of the universe.

Egypt was a polytheistic nation and the Israelites had become accustomed to worshipping the God of their fathers right alongside the false gods of Egypt. The Egyptian gods were worthless and impotent, but when the Israelites met Yahweh, He literally shook their world.

When they came out of Egypt, the Israelites were as children who needed to be educated in the things of God. This was their first lesson in understanding the things of the One True God:

"You shall have no other gods before Me." *(Exodus 20:3)*

<u>The First, the Last and Only God</u>

Worshipping only one god was not a totally new concept in the world at that time, but most nations, like Egypt, were polytheistic. There were some peoples, like the Midianites for example, who knew and worshipped the one true God but who were not in Abraham's chosen line. The Israelites were ordered to limit their worship to Yahweh. God alone had delivered His people from Egypt and He had the right to demand their worship and loyalty.

What God meant by this first commandment was that the Israelites were to have no gods *before* Him, *after* Him, *beside* Him, *instead* of Him or *in addition* to Him. He and He alone was worthy of their worship.

While in Egypt, the Israelites were guilty of all of these infractions. Either the truth about God had not come down to them from their fathers or they had lost faith in Him after centuries of abuse at the hands of the Egyptians. In any case, the Israelites became acquainted with the false gods of Egypt and eventually lusted after them. Such spiritual adultery is detestable to God.

<u>False gods and Real Plagues</u>

The miracles of the ten plagues that God brought upon Egypt had two purposes:

- To convince Pharaoh to give the Israelites their freedom.
- To individually defeat Egypt's false gods.

If God's only reason for bringing the plagues on Egypt was to convince Pharaoh to free the Israelites, He could have simply cut to the chase and gone directly to the tenth plague. But He wanted to demonstrate His power and superiority over the Egyptian gods that had held such an appeal to the Israelites. With just a word, God changed the water of the Nile to blood (Exodus 7:17-18) and the god of the Nile was unable to reverse it. One goddess, Heqt, had the body of a woman and the head of a frog. She was probably hopping mad that not only was she powerless to rid the land of the frogs God had sent, but Pharaoh's magicians only made matters worse by bringing up even more of the critters (Exodus 8:5-7)! One by one, Egypt's false gods were crushed under the power of the God of Israel.

Although the Israelites had witnessed not only the miracles of the plagues but the many miracles associated with their journey through the desert, God knew that it would still be necessary to constantly remind them that He alone was their God and they were to have no other. Thus, the first commandment came into being.

So the first commandment told the Israelites *whom* they were to worship, but what about *how* they were to worship? The second commandment answers that question:

"You shall not make for yourself an idol or any likeness of what is in heaven above or on the earth beneath or in the waters under the earth. You shall not worship them or serve them; for I, the LORD your God, am a jealous God…" *(Exodus 20:4-6)*

While the second commandment stands on its own, it can also be seen as a refinement and a continuation of the first commandment. God is providing a further definition of what He considers to be unacceptable worship, for the Israelites had already shown their propensity for following after false idols.

By definition, an idol is a representation or symbol of an *object of worship*. God was not expressing His dislike for artwork. He was ordering His people not to worship any image created in gold or silver or stone or wood that was created by man for that purpose. He was ordering them not to worship anyone or anything except Him.

The Israelites were used to having physical objects to represent the gods they worshipped. In fact, even while Moses was still on the mountain, the Israelites decided they needed a physical representation of Yahweh that they could bow down to. They convinced Aaron to make a golden calf (Exodus 32:1-4) that they could carry before them. In their minds, they were not rejecting God; they were simply creating a physical representation of Yahweh that they could see and touch.

The problem is that God cannot be represented by any physical object. His awesomeness was beyond the comprehension of the Israelites who were still trying to get to know Him. The reason God gave the Israelites the Mosaic Law, including the Ten Commandments, was so they could get to know who He was and what He expected of them. It was to teach them His perfect standards. It would be a long, slow and painful learning process.

Jealous of Me?

Some might think it strange that God said He was the jealous type. According to Merriam-Webster, the word *jealous* means (1) intolerant of unfaithfulness, (2) hostile toward a rival and (3) vigilant in guarding a possession.

Considering the actual definition of the word *jealous*, it certainly seems like the right word to describe the way God felt about the Israelites. He had already warned them He would not tolerate unfaithfulness and to get rid of those idols. Pharaoh would certainly agree that God was hostile toward a rival. And no one can doubt that God was vigilant in guarding His possession Israel.

The word *jealous* carries a negative connotation because we often hear it used to describe envy, and it implies anger and bitterness. At first blush, when we hear God say that He is a jealous God, it makes us wonder what kind of god would admit to such a thing. Would such a god be small and petty? Oprah Winfrey once said that after reading that passage, she decided she didn't want anything to do with a jealous god. It is unfortunate that people jump to that conclusion without doing a little research, because it is true that in both the Old and New Testaments, the

114

word translated as *jealous* can also rightly be translated as *zealous* and that seems to bring greater understanding to those verses.

In any case, God was serious about claiming the Israelites as His own people. And the Israelites soon learned that He meant what He said.

The Christian Perspective

A huge portion of the New Testament is all about the fact that Christians are not under the Law, have no responsibility to the Law and are not saved by the Law (Galatians 5:1). But does that mean the Ten Commandments, being part of the Law, have nothing to teach us? Absolutely not! God does not change and there is great value and insight that we can gain into His attributes and personality by looking at the Ten Commandments.

So what do these first two commandments tell Christians about God?

- They tell us that He is a God who saves. He sent Moses to save the Israelites from bondage to Pharaoh. He sent Jesus Christ to save us from bondage to sin.
- They tell us that because God redeemed the Israelites from slavery, He demanded their loyalty and worship. Jesus Christ redeemed us from slavery to sin and He reminded His disciples that they must love Him more than they loved their mother, father, sister, brother, more even than life itself (Luke 14:26).
- They tell us that God hates idolatry (1 Corinthians 10:14) and the spiritual adultery it brings. Warnings against idolatry abound in the New Testament. In his missionary travels, the apostle Paul constantly encountered idolatry in the pagan world and his epistles repeatedly warn of its sinfulness (Ephesians 5:5; Galatians

5:20; Colossians 3:5; 1 Corinthians 12:2; 2 Corinthians 6:16). Today we live in a "me-centered" world where we are our own god. Idolatry is a heart condition that causes us to replace God with self-centeredness, greed, pride, celebrities, sports, expensive cars and homes, our pets, our work, and our own image. Whether we realize it or not, we bow down to these things when we let the pursuit of them replace God in our lives. How can we know what our idols are?

> # Our idols are the things in our lives that, if lost, would make us feel like our lives were no longer worth living; things whose loss would make us feel empty and worthless.

Unfortunately, idolatry is alive and well in the 21st century. Jesus said that no man can serve two masters (Matthew 6:24). It's time for Christians today to choose God as their one and only Lord and Master.

LESSON 2–SUMMARY

READ

Genesis 46:26-27, Exodus 1:15-17, Exodus 6:2-3, Exodus 20:3, Exodus 7:17-18, Exodus 8:5-7, Exodus 20:4-6, Exodus 32:1-4, Galatians 5:1, Luke 14:26, 1 Corinthians 10:14, Ephesians 5:5, Galatians 5:20, Colossians 3:5, 1 Corinthians 12:2, 2 Corinthians 6:16, Matthew 6:24

REFLECT

What did the Israelites know about God before the exodus?

_____

_____

_____

How were the Israelites accustomed to worshipping while they were still in bondage?

_____

_____

_____

What were two reasons God brought the ten plagues on Egypt?

_____

_____

_____

What is the main difference between the first and second commandments?

_____

_____

_____

What is idolatry? How can we know what our idols are?

_____

_____

_____

REMEMBER

The Israelites knew *of* God but they did not really *know* God. They did not have written Scriptures to teach them about God and whatever they knew was handed down to them orally.

Egypt was a polytheistic nation which means they worshipped many gods. The Israelites also began worshipping the false gods of Egypt, perhaps because they knew so little about Yahweh, the God of their fathers.

God sent the ten plagues on Egypt not only to convince Pharaoh to free the Israelites but to individually defeat the Egyptian gods. He wanted the Israelites to see His power and superiority over the false gods.

The first commandment tells the Israelites *whom* they were to worship, and the second commandment told them *how* to worship.

Idolatry is when we worship anything or anyone else besides the one true God. Our idols are the things in our lives that, if lost, would make us feel like our lives were no longer worth living.

Seeking Son Light

Section 2
The Ten Commandments

Lesson 3
Name Above All Names

How do we abuse Thy Name? Let me count the ways.

Section 2: The Ten Commandments
Lesson 3: Name Above All Names

Commandment 3: Do not take the name of the Lord your God in vain.

What does it mean to take the name of the Lord in vain?

We often hear that phrase used in a statement such as, "His efforts to stop the fight were in vain." We know in this context, the term "in vain" means unsuccessful, but that definition does not fit the third commandment.

The term "vain" also means "idle, worthless or useless" and when we consider this definition, the meaning of the third commandment comes into focus. God is commanding His people not to use His name in a disrespectful manner. Stating the commandment in this way helps clarify the meaning:

Do not use the name of the LORD your God disrespectfully.

Sadly many people today refuse to comply with this commandment.

<u>What's In A Name?</u>

In ancient times, a person's name was much more than a simple tag used for identification. It had meaning beyond that, such as a person's nature, essence and reputation. A name answered the question, "What are you?" as much as it answered the question, "Who are you?" Even today, it is common to hear someone refer to a person's "good name". In the business world, there is an accounting term called "good will". It refers to monetary value that can be placed on a company's good reputation.

In an earlier lesson, these verses were mentioned:

> # God spoke further to Moses, "I am the LORD and I appeared to Abraham, to Isaac and to Jacob as God Almighty, but by My name the LORD I did not make myself known to them. *(Exodus 6:2-3)*

A study of the book of Genesis shows that God's personal name Jehovah was used more than 160 times, so obviously Abraham, Isaac and Jacob *knew* His name. However, what they apparently did <u>not</u> know was the *meaning* of His name. The meaning of the name Jehovah (the Hebrew version of which is Yahweh – pronounced Yaw'way) is "He brings into existence whatever exists." This name speaks to the fact that God is eternal, omnipotent, and the Creator of the universe.

Through the miracles of the plagues (Exodus 7:4 / Exodus 11:10), Jehovah was able to demonstrate His authority over the false gods, over Pharaoh and over nature itself. The Red Sea parted on His authority (Exodus 14:16-18), water came forth from a rock (Exodus 17:5-6) and enemies were defeated (Exodus 17:8-13). By the time they came to Mount Sinai, the Israelites had come to understand and respect Jehovah and they *knew* Him.

What did the third commandment mean to the Israelites? How did they misuse the name of the Lord? Perhaps the Israelites were being warned against perjury, since invoking God's name in an oath was considered a guarantee of a person's truthfulness; it was intended to strengthen a person's statement or promise. Vows were taken very seriously and the implication was that breaking a vow would invoke God's punishment on the oath-breaker. In fact, the story of Jephthah describes exactly how seriously a vow was to be taken. His careless vow led to the death of his own daughter (Judges 11:29-40).

Remember too that the Israelites had a connection to the occult through their worship of Egypt's false gods. The first and second commandments were intended to put a stop to that worship, and the third commandment carried its own warning not to use God's name in any magical incantations.

Finally, they were being warned not to use God's name in a casual or blasphemous manner such as using it as an exclamation of surprise or as a curse.

The Christian Perspective

How do we abuse Thy Name? Let me count the ways.

The misuse of God's name today is appalling and so common that we are at risk of being desensitized about the disrespect it represents.

Probably the most obvious and common misuse of God's name is when we hear it used as a curse word. And this phenomenon seems to be unique to Christianity. Never have we heard a Buddhist use Buddha's name as a curse word, or Muslims misuse Muhammad's name in that manner.

People often use God's name when they are shocked or surprised. This is a misuse of His name. No one ever says, "Oh my Devil!" when they are shocked or surprised.

Another obvious misuse of His name is that our culture mocks God (Galatians 6:7). Such references to Him imply that He is worthless and has no value. The Internet contains such perverse and disgusting material concerning our precious Savior that it cannot even be described here.

Sometimes the misuse and disrespect of God's name is less obvious.

When a person claims to be a Christian but his life does not prove that claim, then that person is misrepresenting Christ's name and reputation, and thus is taking His name in vain. *(Mark 7:6)*

Perhaps he attends church regularly but refuses to give up his sinful lifestyle. He believes he can hide his sin from his fellow church members, and perhaps he can, but he cannot hide them from God who sees everything.

Then there is the person who makes a promise to God but fails to keep the promise. "Oh God, if you will do this then I will do that." As soon as we get what we want, we quickly push God out of the picture. We have no respect for the promise we made to Him, although He never forgets

His promises to us (2 Corinthians 1:19-21). This too is taking the name of the Lord in vain because our actions show that we place little value in His work in our lives.

Just as in the days of Moses, when we take an oath in the name of the Lord, then we are obligated to keep it. Think about the oath that citizens are required to take when testifying in court: "Do you promise to tell the truth, the whole truth and nothing but the truth, *so help you God?"* This is a solemn oath and if we fail to keep it, we will incur not only a charge of perjury but we will incur God's wrath as well. Jesus warns that we should let our "yes be yes and our no be no". To feel the need to strengthen it with an oath is from the devil (Matthew 5:36-37).

This commandment contains a warning:

"...for the Lord will not leave him unpunished who takes His name in vain." *(Exodus 20:7)*

These words should strike fear in the hearts of those who disrespect and misuse the name of the Lord, but why don't they? How can people disregard a warning so plainly stated?

Perhaps it is because people are not judged immediately for their sins. They see the Scripture that says they will be punished for misusing God's name, but they misuse it anyway and what happens? Nothing.

But remember: justice delayed is not justice denied (Matthew 12:36). Consider this example:

A motorist speeds through a school zone on his way to work, noticing that children are walking to school. He does not notice the police car sitting around the corner until the officer stops the speeder and immediately issues a ticket. This driver does not have to wait long for his judgment!

On another day, the motorist approaches the school zone and specifically looks for the police car. Certain the police car is not there, he speeds through the school zone again. What he does not notice is the traffic camera that records his speed and captures his license plate number. Although he does not receive his judgment immediately, judgment is coming nevertheless, in the form of a ticket received through the mail!

God is patient and gives us time to acknowledge our sins and repent (2 Peter 3:9). This includes the sin of using His name in a disrespectful and inappropriate manner. We often do not immediately suffer the consequences of our sin but that does not mean we will not suffer the consequences at all.

The sin of a true born-again Christian is covered by Christ's blood. But someone who truly loves Christ will not intentionally misuse or disrespect the name of the Savior or the Father.

God's name should be used with care. It should be used in prayer, teaching and ministering. Any other use should be considered carefully before His name is uttered.

LESSON 3–SUMMARY

READ

Exodus 6:2-3, Exodus 7:4 thru 11:10, Exodus 14:16-18, Exodus 17:5-6, Exodus 17:8-13, Judges 11:29-40, Galatians 6:7, Mark 7:6, 2 Corinthians 1:19-21, Matthew 5:36-37, Exodus 20:7, Matthew 12:36, 2 Peter 3:9

REFLECT

What does it mean to take God's name in vain?

_____

_____

_____

What are some ways people today misuse or disrespect God's personal name?

_____

_____

_____

We know that Abraham, Isaac and Jacob all used God's personal name, so what is meant by the statement in Exodus 6:2-3 when God said that by His name the LORD, He did not make Himself known to them?

_____

_____

_____

What does the Bible say will happen to those who take God's name in vain?

_____

_____

_____

Why doesn't God judge sin immediately? What does that mean to us?

_____

_____

_____

REMEMBER

To take God's name in vain means to use His name disrespectfully or mockingly. It reflects a worthless, foolish, prideful and irreverent attitude toward Him.

People today use God's name carelessly and without thought. His name is often used as a curse word or as a way of expressing surprise. Claiming to be a Christian but not living a Christian life is also a way of taking His name in vain. God's name should be used with care. It should be used in prayer, teaching and ministry. Any other use should be considered carefully before His name is uttered.

Although Abraham, Isaac and Jacob *knew* God's personal name, they did not understand the *meaning* of His name. The name Jehovah means, "He brings into existence whatever exists." Through His miracles and displays of power during the exodus, God demonstrated the true meaning of His name.

God promises to punish those who take His name in vain.

God does not judge sin immediately because He is patient and does not want any to perish. To us, this means we need to acknowledge our sin and repent. Those who refuse will face God's judgment and wrath.

Seeking Son Light

Section 2
The Ten Commandments

Lesson 4

Remember the Sabbath

"This is a sign between Me and you throughout your generations."

Section 2: The Ten Commandments
Lesson 4: Remember the Sabbath

4th Commandment: Remember the Sabbath, to keep it holy..

The concept of a Sabbath day was established immediately after the work of creation was done. God worked for six days to create the heavens and the earth, and He rested on the seventh day. He blessed that day and made it holy, thus setting it apart for Himself (Genesis 2:3).

The word "Sabbath" is not used in this passage nor is there a commandment to observe the day. However this text establishes the foundation upon which all other commandments concerning the Sabbath are based.

What? Manna Again?

When the Israelites left Egypt, they left behind their status as slaves and received the status of Favored-People-Of-God. Instead of receiving abuse at the hands of the Egyptian slave masters, they received blessings from the hands of God.

They hadn't been on the road for long when the Israelites started complaining. They complained about everything. At one point, they even complained that God hadn't just killed them in Egypt; instead He had brought them to the middle of the desert with nothing to eat (Exodus 16:3). God promised to provide for them but along with that provision, He would test their obedience (Exodus 16:4).

God caused bread (called *manna*) to fall from heaven for six days out of seven. He told the people that for five days, they should gather only as much manna as they could eat that day but not to leave any until the next day. However on the sixth day, they were to do exactly the opposite and gather enough for both the sixth and seventh day. God told the people they were not to go out on the seventh day to gather manna because there wouldn't be any (Exodus 16:27).

Some of the people did not follow His instructions and gathered enough manna to feed their families for two days. They soon discovered that if the manna was left until the following day, it spoiled and bred worms (Exodus 16:20). However, the extra manna gathered on the sixth day did not spoil. It remained fresh so it could be eaten on the seventh day (Exodus 16:24).

Those who went out on the seventh day to gather manna found none and God said that no man was to go out of his place on the seventh day (Exodus 16:29).

So this was the way God introduced the Israelites to the concept of the Sabbath. This was also the first time the word "Sabbath" was used (Exodus 16:23-30). God blessed the seventh day and made it holy. His blessing and sanctification of the seventh day was based on His day of rest after creation. Because it was holy to the Lord, the Israelites were instructed to observe it.

God did two things to set apart the seventh day for the Israelites:

- He caused manna not to fall from heaven on the seventh day.
- He caused the manna gathered on the sixth day to remain fresh.

In Exodus 16, the people were simply told not to gather manna on the seventh day and that no man was to go out of his place on that day. Further instructions for observing the Sabbath would soon be given.

The giving of the Ten Commandments is described beginning in Exodus 20. The fourth commandment concerns the Sabbath:

Remember the Sabbath, to keep it holy
(Exodus 20:8)

The Israelites were told to *remember* the Sabbath; that is, they were to look back to a prior event for the basis of this commandment. The original basis for the Sabbath was God's rest on the seventh day after He completed His work at creation. In addition, they could look back to God's prior commandment in Exodus 16 which prohibited them from gathering manna on the seventh day.

They are also told to keep the Sabbath holy. This required them to dedicate the day to God in remembrance of His sanctification of the seventh day.

Read Exodus 20:9-11 where the commandment continues. Originally, the Israelites were simply instructed not to gather manna on the seventh day, but the commandment is now expanded to prohibit all work. And not only were the Israelites themselves to abstain from work, their children, their servants, their cattle and even sojourners who were staying with them, were also prohibited from doing work of any kind on the seventh day.

In Exodus 31, the Israelites are once again reminded of the importance of the Sabbath. The tone of the commandment in this chapter is much more direct and emphatic. It is obvious that God is not *suggesting* obedience from His people in observing the Sabbath; He is *demanding* it. The exact wording of this section of Scripture differs somewhat from the wording used in the giving of the fourth commandment.

…You shall surely observe My Sabbaths; for this is a sign between Me and you throughout your generations, that you may know that I am the LORD who sanctifies you. *(Exodus 31:13)*

This passage indicates that observation of the Sabbath was to be extended for all time as a sign between God and the Israelites throughout all generations. He also refers to "MY" Sabbath, again recalling His day of rest after creation (Exodus 31:17).

Perhaps the most significant difference between the commandment as stated in Exodus 20 and in Exodus 31 is that the death penalty has been put on the table.

Therefore you are to observe the Sabbath, for it is holy to you. Everyone who profanes it shall surely be put to death; for whoever does any work on it, that person shall be cut off from among his people. For six days work may be done, but on the seventh day there is a Sabbath of complete rest, holy to the LORD; whoever does any work on the Sabbath day shall surely be put to death. *(Exodus 31:14-15)*

The Sabbath of the Land

Not only did God make a provision for the people to observe a day of rest, but He made a provision for the land to rest as well (Leviticus 25:2-6). The people were to work the land for six years and then allow it to remain dormant on the seventh year. They were not to sow or harvest, prune the vineyards nor gather the grapes.

The people were allowed to eat whatever the land produced but they could not sell it for profit. The poor were allowed to go into the fields and gather all they could eat and the cattle and other animals were to have free access to the land as well.

If the people were obedient to God's commandments, He would provide enough food from the harvest in the sixth year to carry over for another three years (Leviticus 25:20-22)!

Why were the instructions for observing the Sabbath expanded to include the land? There were actually several reasons:

- God wanted to remind the people that He owned the land; they were merely the caretakers of it.

- It provided food for the poor. People could pick the fruit and grain for eating but not for selling.
- It was good for the land. Even agronomists today understand that leaving the land dormant for a season is the best way to revitalize and nourish it.

You Were Serious?

On the heels of Leviticus 25 comes Leviticus 26 which describes the curses God would pile upon the people if they failed to observe His commandments. God began by describing the blessings He would bestow on the people if only they would obey. He promised rains in their season so the land would produce its crop. The people would live in peace and be secure in the land. They would have plenty to eat and harmful beasts would be eliminated. God promised to make the people fruitful and multiply them, and He promised to make His dwelling place with them (Leviticus 26:1-13).

But just as God promised blessings for the people's obedience, He promised curses for disobedience. He would bring consumption and fever to the people to remove their strength. The rains would be withheld so the land would be like bronze and would not yield a crop. There would be pestilence and famine, wild beasts and terror. Their enemies would rule over them. God promised to make the land desolate so even their enemies would be appalled over it. He promised to scatter the people among the nations and lay waste to their cities (Leviticus 26:14-33).

Apparently the people did not believe what God said because these prophecies were fulfilled when the nation of Israel was exiled to Babylon.

We are told that Israel's punishment would last for seventy years (2 Chronicles 36:20-21). We are also told why.

...to fulfill the word of the Lord by the mouth of Jeremiah, until the land had enjoyed its Sabbaths.

The Israelites entered the Promised Land in approximately 1,400 B.C. and were deported to Babylon beginning around 600 B.C. This means the people were in the land for 800 years or so before they were sent off into exile to Babylon. During that time, they did not consistently observe the Sabbath of the land according to God's direction.

The seventy years of captivity is related to the land's lost Sabbaths. The Jews apparently failed to observe the Sabbath for 490 years (70 x 7 = 490). This means they were obedient for at least part of the time they were in the land.

God's commandments were not optional to the Israelites. What do they mean for us today?

<u>The Christian Perspective</u>

The Sabbath was a sign of the covenant between God and the Israelites (Exodus 31:12-13; 16-17) and it does not apply to the church today, although some Christians disagree with this conclusion.

The Sabbath was never intended for the church. Evidence of this can also be found in the fact that nine of the Ten Commandments are repeated in the New Testament. It is the fourth commandment alone that is not given in the New Testament. However, that does not mean Christians cannot keep the *spirit* of the Sabbath, and in fact we should. John tells us to worship in spirit and in truth (John 4:23). When we come together to worship, we are honoring God as the Creator just as the Israelites did. By keeping the *spirit* of the Sabbath, Christians distinguish themselves from the world, and as modern so-called Christian leaders continue to dilute the true gospel message, this becomes even more important. We also enjoy the rest that we have been given in Christ; that is, rest from the works required by the Law.

LESSON 4 – SUMMARY

READ

Genesis 2:3, Exodus 16:3, Exodus 16:4, Exodus 16:27, Exodus 16:20, Exodus 16:24, Exodus 16:29, Exodus 16:23-30, Exodus 20:8, Exodus 20:9-11, Exodus 31:13, Exodus 31:17, Exodus 31:14-15, Leviticus 25:2-6, Leviticus 25:20-22, Leviticus 26:1-13, Leviticus 26:14-33, 2 Chronicles 36:20-21, Exodus 31:12-13, Exodus 31:16-17, John 4:23

REFLECT

When was the first Sabbath day? Why did God bless that day and make it holy?

_____

_____

_____

According to Exodus 16, how were the people to observe the Sabbath?

_____

_____

_____

What additional elements were added to the Sabbath observance in Exodus 20?

_____

_____

_____

What change had been made in the Sabbath observance as stated in Exodus 31?

_____

_____

_____

Why did God give the land its own Sabbath?

_____

_____

_____

What determined the length of time the Israelites would have to remain in captivity in Babylon?

_____

_____

_____

Are Christians today required to observe the Sabbath? Why or why not?

_____

_____

_____

REMEMBER

After God created the heavens and the earth in six days, He rested on the seventh day. He blessed that day and made it holy because His work of creation was done. Although the word "Sabbath" is not used in this text in Genesis 2:3, this represented the first Sabbath day.

In Exodus 16, the people were only required to stay in their places and not go out to gather manna.

In Exodus 20, the requirements for observance of the Sabbath had been expanded to prohibit all types of work. The Israelites, their children, their servants, their cattle and sojourners (aliens) who were staying with them were also prohibited from doing any kind of work on the seventh day.

The main difference in the way the commandment is stated in Exodus 31 is that for anyone violating the Sabbath, the death penalty was given.

God gave the land its own Sabbath to remind the people that He owned the land; they were merely the caretakers of it. It also provided food for the poor and it was good for the land.

The people failed to keep the Sabbath of the land for 490 years, meaning the land did not receive its Sabbaths for 70 years. Thus, the people remained in captivity in Babylon for 70 years in order to give the land its Sabbath rest.

Christians today are not required to observe the Sabbath because it was a sign of the covenant between God and the Israelites. However, Christians can observe the spirit of the Sabbath by coming together to worship and to honor God as the Creator.

Seeking Son Light

Section 2
The Ten Commandments

Lesson 5
Honor Father and Mother

Train up a child in the way he should go, and even when he is old he will not depart from it.

Section 2:   The Ten Commandments
Lesson 5:   Honor Father and Mother

Commandment #5: Honor your father and your mother, that your days may be long upon the land which the LORD has given you.

Beginning with the fifth commandment, we see a change in the focus of God's directives. The first four commandments deal with our relationship with God:

1.   You shall have no other gods before Me.
2.   You shall not worship false idols.
3.   You shall not take the name of the LORD your God in vain.
4.   Remember the Sabbath day, to keep it holy.

The fifth through the tenth commandments deal with our relationships with each other.

One Nation Under God

God had been in the process of creating the nation of Israel since He first met with Abraham centuries before. When they entered Egypt in search of food during a famine, Jacob's family consisted of seventy men (Genesis 46:26-27). Seventy men do not a nation make. But some 400 years later, the number of men surpassed 600,000 and along with the women and children, more than 2 million people left Egypt in the exodus (Exodus 12:37). Now that's a nation!

As Americans, we are familiar with the Constitution of the United States. It creates the manner and structure of our government, guarantees our personal freedoms, regulates commerce, provides for national security and, without exaggeration, controls nearly every aspect of our daily lives. Our form of government is called a *republic*.

The nation of Israel's form of government was called a *theocracy*. In such a government, official policy was provided through immediate divine guidance or by officials who were regarded as divinely guided. God Himself was recognized as the head of the nation of Israel and He governed through divine guidance given to Moses. The Laws that came from God through Moses to the nation of Israel were not limited to religious and ceremonial laws. They contained the regulations for all aspects of the Israelites' daily life (Exodus 21-23).

Ask Not What Your Country Can Do For You...

The final six of the Ten Commandments define the areas of human behavior that have the greatest impact on a society:

5. Honor your father and mother
6. Do not murder
7. Do not commit adultery
8. Do not steal
9. Do not lie
10. Do not covet

God did not arrange these commandments haphazardly. His primary concern was to give the fledgling nation of Israel the greatest chance for success. It is easy to see how the failure to comply with the last five commandments could create roadblocks to peace and cooperation among a people trying to live and work together as a new nation. In order for the nation as a whole to be strong and successful, the people needed to possess certain qualities that would identify them as God's own people:

- Respect for authority
- Loyalty
- Obedience
- High moral standards

Adherence to these principles required that the people took responsibility for their own actions, had respect for one another and were obedient to those in authority.

In the fifth commandment, God is telling us that the appropriate place for these qualities to be taught is within the family. He is also telling us that strong families combine to make strong nations. Perhaps that was why the penalty for violating this commandment was death (Exodus 21:15, Exodus 21:17, Deuteronomy 21:18-21).

Allowing disrespectful behavior to continue not only made for a dysfunctional family but it eroded the strength and quality of the nation as well.

The Christian Perspective

The fifth commandment is not only for small children; it applies to adults as well (Matthew 15:5-9). Even one well advanced into his golden years and whose biological parents died decades ago is called to be obedient to his Heavenly Father. Disobedient children grow up to be disobedient adults. Learning at an early age that we must be obedient to God and be respecters of authority can help us avoid a lifetime of strife and sorrow.

The character traits that dictate a person's conduct are formed at a very early age (Colossians 3:20). Every experience a child has contributes to the formation of his personality and his ability to successfully interact with others. Parents who allow their children to run amok and have their own way are doing them a great injustice.

> # "He who withholds his rod hates his son, but he who loves him disciplines him diligently." *(Proverbs 13:24)*

The World's Oldest Profession: Parenting

Adam and Eve were the first parents to experience the heartbreak and sorrow a strong willed and disobedient child can bring to a family, but they certainly were not the last. Before Eve was tricked by the serpent, she and Adam actually walked with God and knew firsthand of His goodness. They also learned the hard way that disobedience has a terrible consequence, a lesson they undoubtedly taught their children in an effort to help them avoid the same fate.

If it was difficult for Adam and Eve to teach their children to honor and obey God, how much more difficult is that task today? Our society glorifies that which is vile, depraved, disgusting, evil, shameful and sinful. We are overwhelmed by graphic sights and sounds on television and in movies, music, magazines and advertising. Corruption abounds in politics and big business. Our government has decreed that it is legal to kill unborn children. And this is the culture into which we are releasing our children.

What can help parents prepare their children to face this gauntlet? The best "how to" parenting book of all time is the Bible. The book of Proverbs is especially appropriate for this challenge.

A child's mind is like a sponge and children can absorb a vast amount of information. A parent should not underestimate a child's ability to understand and memorize teachings found in the Proverbs. This provides a solid foundation upon which other biblical principles can be built and which the child will use throughout his life.

> ## "Train up a child in the way he should go, and even when he is old he will not depart from it." *(Proverbs 22:6)*

The Beginning of Wisdom

Children must be taught that God is real. (Hebrews 11:6) He exists and He sees and knows everything. Even if something is done in secret, God still sees it. A child might think that just because no one is watching, he can take something that does not belong to him, and no one will know. God will know. *"The fear of the Lord is the beginning of knowledge; fools despise wisdom and instruction."* (Proverbs 1:7)

God always punishes sin. (John 5:28-29) Often times, we do not face immediate judgment for our sin and that makes us falsely believe that we will get away with our folly. That is not true. There is always a consequence to sin.

Children learn from what they see and hear. (Deuteronomy 6:5-7) The best way to teach a child to love and respect God is for the parents themselves to be obedient to God's will. When children witness their parents choosing to follow biblical principles, then they too will respect the Bible's teachings as they begin making their own decisions.

Parents must begin with the Biblical teaching that their child is a sinner. (Proverbs 22:15) All humans have inherited a sinful nature that makes us disrespectful, stubborn, rebellious and self-centered. In our natural state, we do not even have the capacity for goodness. Most parents believe their children are angels but the truth is they are sinners. Only the Bible can help shape a child's will and give him the best opportunity to recognize and resist the lies that cause the downfall of many.

The parents must win every battle. (Proverbs 29:17) As is true for every human being, a child's will is corrupted by sin. In our natural state, we are all self-centered and foolish. Using knowledge and discipline parents must train the child to control his will so he can learn to make wise decisions on his own. *"Do not withhold discipline from a child; if you punish them with the rod, they will not die. Punish them with the rod and save them from death."* (Proverbs 23:13-14, NIV)

LESSON 5–SUMMARY

READ

Genesis 46:26-27, Exodus 12:37, Exodus 21-23, Exodus 21:15, Exodus 21:17, Deuteronomy 21:18-21, Matthew 15:5-9, Colossians 3:20, Proverbs 13:24, Proverbs 22:6, Hebrews 11:6, Proverbs 1:7, John 5:28-29, Deuteronomy 6:5-7, Proverbs 22:15, Proverbs 29:17, Proverbs 23:13-14

REFLECT

Why did God place the commandment to honor our parents above the remaining commandments? (Do not murder, do not commit adultery, do not steal, do not lie, do not covet.)

_____

_____

_____

Why was the penalty so severe (death) for breaking the fifth commandment?

_____

_____

_____

What might one expect from a disobedient child when that child reaches adulthood?

_____

_____

_____

What are some things parents can keep in mind while training their children using biblical principles?

_____

_____

_____

REMEMBER

God's people should possess certain qualities such as obedience, respect for authority and loyalty. The best place for a person to learn these character traits is in the family.

The penalty for breaking the fifth commandment was very severe because dysfunctional and weak families erode the quality and strength of the nation.

A disobedient and disrespectful child will most likely grow into a disobedient and disrespectful adult.

Parents should remember these principles: (1) Children must be taught that God is real. (2) God always punishes sin. (3) Children learn from what they see and hear. (4) Parents must begin with the biblical teaching that their child is a sinner. (5) Parents must win every battle.

Seeking Son Light

Section 2

The Ten Commandments

Lesson 6

Crime and Punishment

If certain killing is identified as *unlawful*, then it logically follows that there must also be *lawful* killing.

Section 2:   The Ten Commandments
Lesson 6:   Crime and Punishment

Commandment #6: "Thou shalt not kill" (King James Version)
Commandment #6 "You shall not murder" (New American Standard)

As any student will attest, learning a new language is very challenging. Traveling abroad and using the language becomes even more difficult when cultural differences are thrown into the mix. A tourist is proud when he is able to tell the taxi driver in his own language to take him to the hotel, but he would be mortified if he knew he actually told the driver to eat his house slippers!

Now imagine putting four thousand years between you and the language you are studying, and it is easy to see how complex certain words or sentences can be. For centuries, this is the challenge that has faced Bible scholars in translating and understanding the Scriptures. There is perhaps no better example of this than in the way the sixth commandment is translated and understood.

The King James Version of the Bible translates the commandment as, "Thou shalt not kill", while the New American Standard version, as well as other modern versions, translate the commandment as "You shall not murder". The difference in the translation of a single word has a tremendous impact on the meaning of this commandment. Many people use this commandment as the basis for their beliefs about capital punishment, war, abortion and killing in self-defense. It is important that we have a clear and proper understanding of its meaning and of God's ultimate purpose in giving this commandment.

<u>Ancient Hebrew 101</u>

One reason the sixth commandment is often misunderstood is because the word translated as "kill" in the King James Bible and as "murder" in more modern translations, can actually be accurately translated either way. The Hebrew word in question is *"ratsach"* and it is the context in which the word is used that determines the proper translation.

This word appears 47 times in the Old Testament and it is variously used to mean "slay", "murder", "kill" and "put to death". There appears to be no unanimous agreement on the meaning of the word in every instance of its usage. However, it is generally agreed among Bible scholars that this simple definition *always* applies:

Ratsach refers to any killing that is done in the manner of a predatory animal, which means either: (1) as an angry reaction to stimulus, or (2) lying in wait, as one waits for prey.

Also remember that Scripture defines Scripture. If there is misunderstanding about one section of Scripture, look for other sections of Scripture that deal with the same subject and the writer's intention becomes clear. It is quite evident from other sections of Scripture that God does not prohibit all killing. In fact, as shown below, there are several references where God actually commands that killing be done.

Critics like to use this example as proof that God contradicts Himself on the subject of killing and murder. A more in depth study of the issue proves there is no contradiction.

The English definition of the word *murder* provides a clue that can be applied to our Bible study. According to the Merriam-Webster Dictionary, *murder* is defined as:

"The <u>unlawful</u> killing of a person especially with malice aforethought."

If certain killing is identified as *unlawful*, then it logically follows that there must also be *lawful* killing. Let's look at some examples of both lawful and unlawful killing.

Lawful Killing

Our modern laws identify certain crimes that qualify for the death penalty. Among these are murder, espionage, and treason. Some countries identify sexual crimes such as rape, incest and adultery as capital crimes, and in Islamic nations, renunciation of the state religion is a crime that is eligible for the death penalty.

Many people today believe that the death penalty is inappropriate regardless of the nature of the crime committed. In fact, for the past several years, the United Nations General Assembly has adopted non-binding resolutions calling for a global moratorium on executions with the goal of eventually abolishing the practice completely.

According to the Bible, the carrying out of an execution by a civil authority is an example of lawful killing. Other examples of lawful killing include killing in war and killing in self-defense.

Read Joshua 7:20-26. This is the story of a man who deliberately defied God's instructions about taking plunder from the city of Jericho. Because of his actions, Israel suffered defeat in a subsequent conflict. When his crime was discovered, the man was put to death by stoning at God's direction.

Read Numbers 15:32-36. This is the account of the Israelites in the wilderness after they had received the Ten Commandments. In direct defiance of God's commandment, a man was discovered collecting firewood on the Sabbath. God instructed Moses to put the man to death.

Both of these accounts show that God believes the death penalty is justified in certain cases. These were capital offenses because both men willfully ignored God's commandments and challenged His authority.

Read Joshua 8:1-25. When the Israelites entered the land of Canaan to take it as their own, God was their Commander-in-Chief. All the Israelites had to do was to be obedient and follow His directions. Although actions such as those described in this account seem very harsh to us, killing is a reality of war.

Read Judges 4:21. This woman did not hesitate to kill the commander of the opposing army when she had the opportunity. God often uses the least likely people to accomplish His work.

These were lawful killings because they were acts of war. God not only approved of the killing in Ai, but He actually directed it. We often do not understand how God works but our duty is to be obedient and trust that He has a plan that works for the good of those who belong to Him *(Romans 8:28)*. When we fail to do what God calls us to do, we are refusing to submit to His authority. That kind of thinking is never right. Acting in defiance of God is never the right decision.

Unlawful Killing

We do not have to go very far into the Old Testament before we find our first example of unlawful killing.

Read Genesis 4:4-8. God did not look upon Cain's offering with favor as He did upon Abel's offering. Cain was angry and jealous because of God's rejection and he took his anger out on Abel.

Read Exodus 2: 11-12. Moses became angry when he saw an Egyptian abusing one of the Hebrew slaves. Moses showed that he knew his actions were wrong because he looked around to be certain no one was watching as he struck the Egyptian down, and also because he tried to hide the body.

These were unlawful killings because the only reason they occurred was because of the anger of the perpetrators. These men took God's role into their own hands to satisfy their anger.

Although these murders were committed before the sixth commandment was even given, both men knew they had crossed a forbidden line. Cain lied when God asked him about Abel's whereabouts, and Moses tried to hide his crime. But the God who sees everything (Hebrews 4:13) knew not only about the murders but also about the heart condition of the murderers.

Read 2 Samuel 11:14-15. Even King David who knew and loved God dearly, allowed his sinful nature to get the best of him as he coveted his neighbor's wife. He was guilty of coveting and adultery and these sins eventually led him to murder.

The stories of these murders show us that God is not only just but He is sovereign and He is merciful. Instead of giving Cain the death penalty, God was merciful and allowed him to live. He placed a mark on him to protect him from suffering the same fate as his brother (Genesis 4:15). God not only did not put Moses to death for his crime, but as we have seen, He used Moses in a great way. King David escaped the death penalty, and in His mercy, God kept the promises He had made to David and sent the Savior of the world through David's line (2 Samuel 7:16).

As we read these passages, we can recognize the same sinful nature in these men that we ourselves possess. Immediately after completion of creation, God said everything was good (Genesis 1:31). But the impact of man's fall still affects us today. Throughout the ages, God has reminded us that He has a plan to save us from our sins. It is impossible to read the Ten Commandments and not marvel at how completely God knows us, knows our nature and knows that we are in no way capable of saving ourselves.

The Christian Perspective

Jesus referred to the sixth commandment in His Sermon on the Mount (Matthew 5:21-22). His explanation of its meaning went far beyond what had been traditionally understood about killing and murder.

When most Christians read Exodus 20:13, "You shall not murder", they feel like they have nailed at least one of the Ten Commandments. Murder is something that, thankfully, most of us will never be guilty of. But Jesus' teaching went beyond the sixth commandment by saying that anyone who was guilty of anger was in danger of judgment. He taught that anger is the seed and murder is the vine. If the seed of anger is not sown, it cannot grow into an all consuming rage that could result in murder. (Ephesians 4:26; James 1:19-20)

Anger is a completely normal, human emotion, a response to both internal and external stimulus. In our stress filled world, anger-causing stimulus is always lurking just around the corner: a traffic jam, a canceled flight, a problem with a boss or co-worker; financial worries. The list goes on.

When we become angry, our bodies actually experience physical changes: our heart rate and blood pressure go up as do our energy hormones and adrenaline. We instinctively respond to anger aggressively. Anger is the natural human response to a threat and it allows us to fight and defend ourselves.

The emotion of anger is not sinful, but it is dangerous.

The reason we know anger in and of itself is not sinful is that the Bible gives us several examples of God's anger, and God does not sin. (Psalm 7:11; 1 Kings 11:9; 2 Kings 17:18; Mark 3:5)

Anger Management

What can we learn from Jesus about dealing with our anger? Jesus taught that nothing was more important than making amends with a person with whom there was a disagreement (Matthew 5:23-24).

Don't be afraid to be the first to say, "I'm sorry" even if you feel that you were wronged. We should forgive others because God forgave us (Colossians 3:13).

Pray for your enemies. Use this conflict as an opportunity for God to bring out the best in you, not the worst. We grow through our trials (Matthew 5:44-45).

Know when to step away. When dealing with a very angry person, often the best action is to simply step away from the situation before it can escalate into a more serious confrontation (Matthew 12:14-15; Matthew 16:4; John 10:39).

Anger is only one reason people commit murder. In Galatians 5:19-21, Paul identifies the deeds of the flesh that place us in danger of losing our souls. Every day we see people who are lost in these sins. And all too often as we listen to the news or read the newspaper, we hear of another murder. How many murders might be avoided if the people involved would pray for their enemies and for themselves, apologize, forgive or simply step away? Until people are willing to follow the model Jesus gave us, we will not know the answer to that question. Sadly, as people continue in their sins, they will learn too late that Paul's warning is true: "…I have forewarned you, that those who practice such things will not inherit the kingdom of God." (1 Corinthians 6:9-10)

LESSON 6–SUMMARY

READ

Joshua 7:20-26, Numbers 15:32-36, Joshua 8:1-25, Judges 4:21, Romans 8:28, Genesis 4:4-8, Exodus 2:11-12, Hebrews 4:13, 2 Samuel 11:14-15, Genesis 4:15, 2 Samuel 7:16, Genesis 1:31, Matthew 5:21-22, Ephesians 4:26, James 1:19-20, Psalm 7:11, 1 Kings 11:9, 2 Kings 17:18, Mark 3:5,Matthew 5:23-24, Colossians 3:13, Matthew 5:44-45, Matthew 12:14-15, Matthew 16:4, John 10:39, 1 Corinthians 6:9-10

REFLECT

Why was it difficult for Bible scholars to translate the sixth commandment?

_____

_____

_____

How can you discover the meaning of a difficult section of Scripture?

_____

_____

_____

What does the English definition of the word "murder" tell us?

_____

_____

_____

How do we know that anger, in and of itself, is not a sin?

_____

_____

_____

Jesus taught about anger in both words and actions. What are some examples we can use to deal with our own anger?

_____

_____

_____

REMEMBER

The Hebrew word translated as "kill" in the King James Bible and as "murder" in more modern translations can accurately be translated either way. It is the context in which the word is used that determines its meaning.

Scripture defines Scripture. When reading a passage that is difficult to understand, find other passages that deal with the same subject and the meaning becomes clear.

The English definition for murder is, "The *unlawful* killing of a person." If some killing is defined as unlawful, then it logically follows that there is also *lawful* killing which would include killing in war, capital punishment and self-defense.

We know that anger in and of itself is not sinful because the Bible gives several examples of God's anger, and God does not sin. However, although anger is not itself a sin, it is a dangerous emotion.

Jesus taught that nothing is more important than making amends with a person with whom there is a disagreement. Making amends is more important than offering a gift on the altar. We should pray for our enemies. If we turn to God in prayer, He can use this conflict as an opportunity to bring out the best in us. Sometimes the best response to anger is to simply step away from the situation. Finally, Jesus taught us to forgive. We should forgive as Jesus forgave.

Seeking Son Light

Section 2
The Ten Commandments

Lesson 7
Do Not Commit Adultery

"For your Maker is your husband – the LORD Almighty is His name – The Holy One of Israel is your Redeemer."

Section 2: The Ten Commandments
Lesson 7: Do Not Commit Adultery

The Joy of Sex

"I slept but my heart was awake. Listen! My lover is knocking. I have taken off my robe; must I put it on again? My lover thrust his hand through the latch opening; my heart began to pound for him….Come, my lover, let us go to the countryside, let us spend the night in the villages. Let us go early to the vineyards to see if the vines have budded; if their blossoms have opened, and if the pomegranates are in bloom, there I will give you my love."

This erotic passage is not from an "X" rated movie, nor is it from a new romance novel. It comes directly from the Bible, specifically from Solomon's book, Song of Songs 5:2-4; 7:11-12, NIV.

As R. Kent Hughes wrote in his commentary on the book of Exodus, "Although God's Word is never pornographic, it is unashamedly erotic. If this comes as an embarrassment to some Christians, it is only because we are more prudish than God is."

Marriage was designed for companionship, intimacy and procreation. One pastor has referred to sexual intimacy as the super glue that holds a marriage together. Have you ever carelessly used super glue? It can be misused and allowed to touch things you never intended to get stuck together. When you try to separate the haphazardly glued-together pieces, often one or both are completely destroyed. At the very least, separation is quite painful.

Today there seems to be a general belief that there is nothing wrong with casual sexual encounters among consenting adults, although many still try to hide their affairs. But nothing is hidden from God (Psalm 33:13). Such immoral actions are in full view of God and they are detestable to Him.

When God created woman, His intention was to create a helper for Adam. He did not have to go to Adam for spare parts (Genesis 2:21-24). He could have created Eve in exactly the same way He created Adam: from the dust of the ground. But instead God chose to use Adam's rib to form Eve, signifying that together, a man and his wife form one complete whole.

As humans, we tend to form our beliefs based on what we want and what we consider to be normal. The problem is that we view our sexual behavior through human eyes. Unless our beliefs are based on biblical truth, we are not right with our Holy God. He is sovereign; He calls the shots.

The Scope of the Seventh Commandment

Scholars agree that the seventh commandment does not limit itself to adultery *per se* but it applies to all sexual sins including fornication, homosexuality, premarital sex and pornography. Some consider adultery to be the greatest sexual sin because it breaks the marriage promise, a promise made in the presence of God. It destroys the trust between a husband and wife. Thus we see that the protection of the institution of marriage is one important reason this commandment was given.

What is Adultery?

The Bible speaks of three types of adultery:

- Physical adultery
- Emotional adultery
- Spiritual adultery

Physical Adultery: Physical adultery is what we typically think of first when we hear the word *adultery*. It is when a married person engages in sexual intercourse with a person to whom he or she is not married. The Bible is full of admonitions against it. See Hebrews 13:4, Proverbs 22:14 and Proverbs 6:26.

Emotional Adultery: In the previous lesson, we learned that Jesus expanded the scope of the sixth commandment which prohibited murder. He said that anyone who was angry with his brother was in danger of judgment. In the same way, He expanded the scope of the seventh commandment concerning adultery. Jesus said that anyone who even looked at a woman lustfully had already committed adultery with her in his heart (Matthew 5:27-28). Jesus meant that it is only a short distance between lusting after someone and acting upon that lust-driven desire to commit adultery.

We need only to look at the story of King David to understand how looking lustfully at a woman quickly escalated to the act of adultery, covetousness and murder.

Even from a young age, David was a man of God. He gained fame when he killed the giant Philistine Goliath and eventually became King of

Israel. He worshipped God and wrote hymns of praise and God promised him that his royal line would continue forever (2 Samuel 7:16).

But David allowed lust to enter his life and it nearly destroyed him. (2 Samuel 11). What do you think King David's advice would be to a man today contemplating a sexual affair with another man's wife? He would advise the man to turn his eyes away from whatever it is he lusts after and not to allow those lustful thoughts to become dangerous, even murderous, actions.

Spiritual Adultery: Spiritual adultery is when God's people are unfaithful to Him by lusting after false gods and idols. God alone is worthy of our worship and praise. He is a jealous God and refuses to share the worship that rightfully belongs to Him (Exodus 20:4).

As a husband cares for his wife, God protected and nurtured the Israelites as they came out of Egypt and formed a new nation. He went before them in battle bringing them victory, and led them to the Promised Land. He provided for their every need and taught them how to be His people. They were as His first love and He was their husband.

> For your Maker is your husband – the LORD Almighty is His name – the Holy One of Israel is your Redeemer; He is called the God of all the earth. *(Isaiah 54:5 NIV)*

But Israel was rebellious and refused to submit to her husband. When she was punished for her unfaithfulness, the people begged God for mercy. (Jeremiah 5:7-9).

In God's eyes, adultery is detestable and He considers it an abomination. Israel was to be pure but she was filthy; she had promised to be faithful but she lusted after false gods and idols. God promised her hope and she killed His Son.

The Christian Perspective

We can say that we are disgusted by the overtly sexual tones used in the advertising and entertainment industries, but do we turn away? Do we boycott the movie theaters? Do we blush? Or are we drawn in, watching to see where all this will lead?

We can say we miss the simpler times when offensive and blasphemous images did not force their way into our living rooms through the television. But the truth is that we can't put the genie back into the bottle.

Truly born-again Christians make up a small percentage of the American population and it seems to be getting smaller every day. What can Christians do to make a difference? How can we be the salt of the earth that Jesus spoke of and let our lights shine into the utter darkness in this country (Matthew 5:13-16)? Perhaps these suggestions will help:

Be vigilant. Recovering alcoholics know if they hang out at taverns and bars, they are at risk of losing their sobriety. Likewise, Christians should avoid the people and places that lead to temptation. They should not put themselves in situations which can lead to actions that are displeasing to God and ultimately, dangerous for themselves. Drunkenness and crude behavior are not characteristics of godly people. They provide great opportunities for sin.

The family computer should not be set up in a secluded place in the house but should be located in a gathering place where there is plenty of traffic and multiple sets of eyes. This eliminates the temptation to view pornography and other unsuitable material.

Seeking emotional support or marital advice from any member of the opposite sex can place both parties in danger of yielding to temptation. Even pastors and biblical counselors are not immune to temptation through prolonged counseling with the opposite sex. A more appropriate option is for an individual to seek counsel from a spiritually mature member of the same sex or a married couple.

Choose carefully. A walk down the aisle is meant to be a once-in-a-life-time event. The marriage partners should think about the fact that this is the first person they will see each morning and the last person they will see at night. And although only two people walk down the aisle, each will actually be gaining an entire family along with their beloved. If the family relationships are not good, conflicts should be worked out before the knot is tied; it is very unlikely the conflicts will work themselves out afterwards. The married couple will spend every holiday, birthday and anniversary with these people for the rest of their lives. It's something to think about.

The potential marriage partners should share a value system. Believers should not marry unbelievers (2 Corinthians 6:14-16). An understanding should be reached beforehand that the husband is the head of the family and the wife is his helper (Ephesians 5:23). Husbands must love their wives as Christ loves the church (Ephesians 5:25) and wives must submit to their husbands as the church submits to Christ *(Colossians 3:18)*.

<u>Marriage is forever</u>. When the going gets tough and it will, remember that marriage is for the long haul. Marriage is a voluntary vow taken before God and He expects that vow to be kept.

<u>Be united in thoughts and actions</u>. Because the relationship between a husband and wife is very similar to the relationship between Christ and His church, it is precious and sacred to God. The family must be structured and operated according to biblical standards and when it is, God will abundantly give His blessings.

<u>Know what the Bible says about adultery</u>. Unrepentant adulterers do not go to heaven (1 Corinthians 6:9-10). God will judge the adulterer (Hebrews 13:4). Adultery is a heart condition (Matthew 15:19). God is willing to forgive the truly repentant adulterer (1 Corinthians 6:11).

Love in a marriage goes deeper than the type of love we feel when we enter into a new romance. That kind of love is thrilling, to be sure. It makes our heart beat a little bit faster and puts a spring in our step. Love in a marriage is self-sacrificing. It is deep and unconditional. Such love is second only to the love we feel for our Savior.

The wedding feast is being prepared. Is the Bridegroom expecting you?

LESSON 7–SUMMARY

READ

Song of Songs 5:2-4, Song of Songs 7:11-12, Psalm 33:13, Genesis 2:21-24, Hebrews 13:4, Proverbs 22:14, Proverbs 6:26, Matthew 5:27-28, 2 Samuel 7:16, 2 Samuel 11, Exodus 20:4, Isaiah 54:5, Jeremiah 5:7-9, Matthew 5:13-16, 2 Corinthians 6:14-16, Ephesians 5:23, Ephesians 5:25, Colossians 3:18, 1 Corinthians 6:9-10, Hebrews 13:4, Matthew 15:19, 1 Corinthians 6:11

REFLECT

What is the overall scope of the seventh commandment and what is one reason it was given?

_____

_____

_____

What are the three types of adultery discussed in the Bible and how are they different from one another?

_____

_____

_____

Why did God create Eve from Adam's rib when He could just as easily have created her from the dust of the earth?

_____

_____

_____

Why is spiritual adultery so detestable to God?

_____

_____

_____

In terms of adultery, why is it important that Christians today be the salt of the earth and the light of the world?

_____

_____

_____

What are some ways Christians can give themselves the best chance for a successful and faithful marriage?

_____

_____

_____

REMEMBER

The seventh commandment is not just about adultery. It prohibits all sexual sins such as fornication, homosexuality, premarital sex and pornography. One reason the seventh commandment was given was to protect the institution of marriage.

The Bible discusses three types of adultery: Physical adultery is sexual intercourse between a married person and a person to whom he or she is not married; emotional adultery is driven by lust; and spiritual adultery is when God's own people are unfaithful to Him with false gods and idols.

One reason God created Eve from Adam's rib was to signify that together, a man and his wife are as one whole and complete person.

Spiritual adultery is detestable to God because He alone is worthy of our praise and worship. He is the one and only true God, a jealous God who is not willing to share the worship that rightfully belongs only to Him.

Christians are Jesus Christ's ambassadors on earth and it is important that they live up to God's standards. Just as Satan our accuser watches, waiting for us to make a mistake, unbelievers watch also. Their own guilt is minimized when they see a Christian fail at keeping God's commandments.

Christians can give themselves the best chance for a successful marriage if they choose their mate carefully. A believer should not marry an unbeliever; each person should live by biblical principles. Understand before getting married that the husband is the head of the wife as Christ is the head of the Church, and the wife is to submit to her husband as the Church submits to Christ. The partners need to agree that arguments or disagreements will not end the marriage, and both partners need to know what the Bible says about adultery.

Seeking Son Light

Section 2
The Ten Commandments

Lesson 8
Be a Good Neighbor

You cannot be a good neighbor if you steal from him, lie to him or covet what he has.

Section 2:   The Ten Commandments
Lesson 8:   Be A Good Neighbor

In the New Testament, Jesus said

"Love your neighbor as yourself."
(Mark 12:31)

In a practical sense, Jesus' statement encompasses the final three commandments given by God to Moses:

- 8th Commandment: You shall not steal (Exodus 20:15)
- 9th Commandment: You shall not give false testimony against your neighbor (Exodus 20:16)
- 10th Commandment: You shall not covet anything that belongs to your neighbor (Exodus 20:17)

You cannot be a good neighbor if you steal from him, lie to him or covet what he has.

Remember, God was in the process of making Israel into a nation. In one way or another, each of the Ten Commandments was meant to bring Israel closer to that goal. God was teaching the people how to worship Him and how to treat one another. The final six commandments in particular were designed to help the people successfully interact with one another and to simply get along. The commandments were to be their standard of conduct in everyday life.

You Shall Not Steal

While the Israelites wandered in the wilderness for forty years, God provided for all their needs. They needed water: God provided water (Exodus 17:5-6). They needed food: God provided food (Exodus 16:4-5; Exodus 16:11-12). They needed rest: God provided rest (Exodus 31:15). Through these acts, God proved that He was trustworthy. All of the good things the Israelites received during that time were direct gifts from God, and that fact was evident to all since they were alone in the desert without resources.

God gave gifts to satisfy the needs of His people. If a gift was stolen by someone else, the person who had originally received the gift was in want once again and the thief was guilty of stealing directly from God. The thief stole the provision God had made for the other person. And by stealing, the thief was also showing that he did not trust God to provide for him.

Stealing By Any Other Name...Well, It's Still Stealing

Unfortunately, stealing is nearly commonplace today and it is seen in every area of our society. Here are just a few of the many examples of stealing:

Burglary, robbery, larceny, hijacking, shop lifting, pick pocketing, embezzlement, extortion, racketeering, and identity theft. Taking supplies from work and items from hotels, hospitals, building sites and churches. Some people refuse to pay taxes, make false claims to receive benefits, falsify time cards, call in sick when they aren't, make long-distance phone calls from work and surf the internet for pleasure. They commit insurance fraud, violate copyright laws, steal intellectual property, and are guilty of plagiarism. Employers force their workers to put in extra time with no extra pay. Corporations manipulate securities through false information, using immoral business practices, price gouging, false advertising and deceptive packaging. The government steals from the people through wasteful and inefficient use of public funds and by accumulating debt with no real intention of repaying it. Credit card companies and lenders charge interest rates that are way too high.

This is not an exhaustive list. Who can read this list and still believe that humans, on their own, have any righteousness in them at all?

You Shall Not Give False Testimony Against Your Neighbor

In the ancient judicial system, people charged with a crime were presumed guilty until they were proven innocent. The penalty for many crimes was death so a defendant's life was on the line. To make matters worse, courts were often willing to convict a person based on the testimony of a single witness and there was no forensic science to prove or disprove his claims. The words of a false witness could mean death for an innocent person.

This is the context in which God gave the ninth commandment.

God's Law required a matter "to be established by two or three witnesses" and in death penalty cases, this became even more important. Therefore, in Israel at least, no one could be sentenced to death based on the testimony of a single witness (Deuteronomy 17:6). In addition, the law stated that if a witness proved to be a liar, he would face the same punishment the accused person would have faced if found guilty (Deuteronomy 19:18-19).

Many people today have lost confidence in the American justice system and indeed, it seems there is less concern about justice and more concern about winning the case at any cost. The focus of everyone involved in the legal system must be to find and maintain the truth, the whole truth and nothing but the truth.

The ninth commandment is about more than giving false testimony at a trial however.

It forbids every form of falsehood and deceit (Exodus 23:1; Psalm 5:5-6). We know this because in the Hebrew language, there are separate words for lying:

- *Shaqar* is the Hebrew term for false testimony.
- *Kachash* is a more general term that refers to any kind of lying.

The word used to state the ninth commandment is *kachash*, referring to all types of lies and deceit.

There are many ways to violate the commandment against lying. There are little white lies and there are big lies: the whoppers and grand deceptions (John 8:44). There are twisting the truth, flatteries and fibs (Romans 16:18). We mislead people, misquote them and take things out of context. We spread rumors, gossip and slander (Romans 1:29). We exaggerate another person's short comings without considering our own. We always tell a story to put ourselves in the best light.

The most serious offense of course is when our lies hurt others. Words are powerful and dangerous and can lead to discord and separation. They can hurt the reputation of others and a reputation is important. Words should be used to build others up, not to tear them down and ruin their reputation (Proverbs 22:1; Psalm 15).

<u>You Shall Not Covet Anything That Belongs To Your Neighbor</u>

Covet is a word that is seldom used these days but the behavior it represents is alive and well. To *covet* is when a person craves or yearns for something that he does not have, especially when he craves something that belongs to another person (Joshua 7:20-22).

We call it chasing the American dream or keeping up with the Joneses, but God calls it coveting.

The tenth commandment is the only one that refers to our having a particular heart condition. All the other commandments are to promote or prohibit specific behaviors, but this one teaches us that God demands inward as well as outward obedience (Deuteronomy 7:25-26). This was illustrated in the way in which the Pharisees viewed the Sabbath. They were able to outwardly keep the Sabbath but their hearts had become so hardened, they failed to see that the Sabbath was made for man, not man for the Sabbath, until Jesus demonstrated it to them (Luke 13:13-15).

Why is coveting so bad that God had to give a commandment to prohibit it? It is because coveting often leads to other sins. King David saw Bathsheba but knew he could not have her. The more he thought about it, the more he wanted her, and eventually he stole her from her husband, lied about it, committed adultery and then committed murder to cover up his sin (2 Samuel 11). Coveting is like a sinkhole filled with quick sand. A person can dance around the edge of it and hope he doesn't fall in, but if he takes one step too close, he is doomed.

Another purpose for the commandment is to teach us once again that on our own, we cannot meet God's standard of righteousness.

His standard of righteousness applies not only to what we do but what we *want* to do.

It proves to us that we are in need of a Savior.

Everything we have and everything we need is provided by God. By coveting what we don't have, we are telling Him that we are not happy with the provision He has made for us. As long as we base our sense of contentment on the things of this world, we will find contentment to be an elusive goal.

The Christian Perspective

Why is it so hard for us to be kind to one another? Why do we have no sense of righteousness when it comes to our dealings with other people? Why is the fruit of the spirit (Galatians 5:22-23) so foreign to many of us?

It is impossible for a born-again Christian to look at his fellow man and not feel a sense of pity, not mourn for the spirit of a man who does not know God (Matthew 5:4).

The unsaved man is stumbling in darkness but refuses to go to the light.

Although he might be miserable in his present state, he does not know another way. Like a dog abused by his master, he is ignorant of the sanctuary that is waiting to accept him.

The Great Commission was not just for those who were present when Christ ascended into Heaven (Acts 1:8). It has now fallen to us to show the unsaved another way to live. We are to lead them to the sanctuary that is Jesus Christ so the Holy Spirit can continue His work. We are the light that will show lost ones the way to Christ (John 3:19). And if our words are not persuasive enough, let our actions do the talking (James 1:22).

God's purpose in giving the Ten Commandments to the Israelites was to set them apart from the pagans and to announce to the world that they were God's own people. He also gave the Commandments to prove to the people that on their own, they were not capable of keeping them.

By telling His disciples to love God with all their hearts and souls and minds, and to love their neighbors as themselves (Mark 12:30-31), Jesus called His followers to keep all of the commandments but one: the commandment to observe the Sabbath. We are to keep the commandments inwardly as well as outwardly, and this is possible only when we allow the Holy Spirit to change us from the inside out. By living out the Great

Commission, we are light to the lost. And like our Good Shepherd, we are not willing to lose a single one.

LESSON 8 – SUMMARY

READ

Mark 12:31, Exodus 20:15-17, Exodus 17:5-6, Exodus 16:4-5, Exodus 16:11-12, Exodus 31:15, Deuteronomy 17:6, Deuteronomy 19:18-19, Exodus 23:1, Psalm 5:5-6, John 8:44, Romans 16:18, Romans 1:29, Proverbs 22:1, Psalm 15, Joshua 7:20-22, Deuteronomy 7:25-26, Luke 13:13-15, 2 Samuel 11, Galatians 5:22-23, Matthew 5:4, Acts 1:8, John 3:19, James 1:22, Mark 12:30-31

REFLECT

Why does this lesson refer to the final three commandments as the "good neighbor" commandments?

_____

_____

_____

What are two reasons why stealing is wrong?

_____

_____

_____

What are some ways that people today steal? In what context was the ninth commandment (Do not give false testimony) given?

_____

_____

_____

In addition to outright lying, what does the ninth commandment also prohibit?

_____

_____

_____

How is the tenth commandment (Do not covet) different from all of the other commandments?

_____

_____

_____

Why is coveting such a dangerous sin?

_____

_____

_____

REMEMBER

The eighth, ninth and tenth commandments can be referred to as the "good neighbor" commandments because a person cannot be a good neighbor if he steals from him, lies to him and covets what he has.

Stealing is wrong for many reasons, but two important reasons are (1) because when a person takes something that belongs to another person, he is stealing the provision God has made for that person and, (2) because the thief is telling God that he does not trust Him to provide for all his needs.

People steal today by taking supplies home from work, falsify time cards, make long distance calls from work and call in sick when they aren't.

Refusing to pay taxes, violating copyright laws and borrowing money with no intention of paying it back are also forms of stealing.

In the ancient legal system, a person could be found guilty of a crime and even be sentenced to death on the testimony of a single witness. God gave this commandment so that the testimony of at least two witnesses was needed to convict a person of a crime.

In addition to outright lying, the ninth commandment also prohibits telling "little white lies", flattery, twisting the truth, misleading people, misquoting them and taking things out of context. Spreading rumors and gossiping are also prohibited under the ninth commandment.

The tenth commandment differs from the other commandments in that it requires inward obedience to God. It teaches us that on our own we cannot meet God's standard of righteousness which applies not only to what we do, but what we *want* to do.

Coveting is a dangerous sin because it often leads to other sins and breaking other commandments. A person covets something that does not belong to him, he steals it, lies about it and perhaps even commits murder to cover up the crime.

Seeking Son Light

Section 2
The Ten Commandments

For further reading...

"Exodus: Saved by God's Glory" by Philip Graham Ryken

"Exodus: The Birth of the Nation" by Bob Deffinbaugh

"Leviticus: Sacrifice and Sanctification" by Bob Deffinbaugh

"The Thomas Ice Collection – The Seventy Weeks of Daniel" by Thomas Ice

"The Way of the Master" by Ray Comfort

Seeking Son Light

Section 3
The Life of Christ

Lesson 1
Before Bethlehem

His goings forth are from long ago,
from the days of eternity.

Section 3: The Life of Christ
Lesson 1: Before Bethlehem

Study any famous person like Julius Caesar, George Washington or Winston Churchill and the appropriate place to begin is with that person's birth. Not so with Jesus Christ.

As the second person of the Triune Godhead (the Trinity) Christ has *always* existed. He is eternal (having infinite duration, endless) and He was pre-existent (He existed before being born as a human infant in Bethlehem.)

Pre-Existent and Eternal

According to Charles C. Ryrie in his *Basic Theology*, "The pre-existence of Christ means that He existed before His birth. For some writers it means that He existed before Creation and before time. But strictly speaking, pre-existence is not synonymous with eternality. Practically speaking, they stand for a similar concept, for a denial of pre-existence almost always includes a denial of eternality and vice versa."

Prior to the early fourth century, there was a school of thought called *Arianism* which denied the Trinitarian doctrine. This concept held that Jesus was the first *created* being and as such, was subordinate to and distinct from the Father. To support their beliefs, the Arians cited John 14:28 where Jesus said, "...the Father is greater than I" and Proverbs 8:22: "The Lord created me at the beginning of His work." These beliefs were in opposition to mainstream theology and were deemed heretical by the First Council of Nicaea in A.D. 325. Even so, the teachings are still present today in some groups such as the Mormons and Jehovah's Witnesses.

In regard to the verses identified above as supporting the Arian beliefs, both have been taken out of context. When properly studied, it is apparent that neither of the verses supports the Arian teachings.

The Eternal Son of God

The doctrine of the eternity of Christ is foundational to the Christian faith. Consider the implications of Christ as a created being:

- *If* Christ is a created being *then* He is not eternal. There is no eternal Trinity.
- *If* Christ is not eternal *then* He cannot be God. God is eternal.
- *If* Christ is not God *then* He cannot be the Creator. Only God can create something from nothing.
- *If* Christ is not God *then* He cannot be our Savior. Only God can forgive sins and we are lost.

We must have a confident belief that Christ is eternal and that He is God. We cannot continue to grow and mature as Christians if our position on this critical doctrine is not rock solid.

In an earlier section in this study, we examined the Bible itself and described the many reasons we can have complete confidence in its teachings, accuracy, truthfulness and reliability. Let us now test our faith in the Bible and discover what it says about Christ and His eternality.

Christ Before Bethlehem

Christ is our best witness as to His pre-existence and eternality. Jesus gave direct evidence that He was pre-existent when He said, "...before Abraham was born, I AM." (John 8:58). The Jews of His day clearly understood Jesus' statement as a reference to Exodus 3:14 in which God identified Himself to Moses as "I AM". They thought Jesus was guilty of blasphemy and they immediately tried to stone Him to death. It never occurred to them that Jesus was telling the truth. Christ told of His former glory that He shared with His Father before His incarnation (John 17:5).

John, the beloved disciple, wrote of Christ:

> "In the beginning was the Word, and the Word was with God, and the Word was God. He was in the beginning with God. All things came into being through Him, and apart from Him nothing came into being that has come into being." *(John 1:1-3)*

Remember, like the other apostles, John had spent three years living with and learning from Jesus, and their last 40 days together were after Christ's resurrection. Just think about the truths that were uncovered for the Apostles during those final days! So when John wrote these things, he was not using his imagination or telling what he *thought* was truth, he was telling what he *knew* was truth, for he had heard it from Jesus Christ Himself.

John also referred to the Father loving Jesus before the foundation of the world (John 17:24).

John the Baptist received a revelation concerning Jesus and he knew that Jesus was the awaited Messiah (John 1:15, 30; Mark 1:7-8).

The apostle Paul wrote that Jesus was the instrument of His Father's plan for the redemption of mankind:

> Blessed be the God and Father of our Lord Jesus Christ, who has blessed us with every spiritual blessing in the heavenly places in Christ, just as He chose us in Him before the foundation of the world. *(Ephesians 1:3-4)*

The prophets knew of His pre-existence. Micah acknowledged this when he wrote…

> His goings forth are from long ago, from the days of eternity. *(Micah 5:2)*

Isaiah also prophesied about the coming Messiah when he made reference to "Wonderful Counselor, Mighty God, Eternal Father, Prince of Peace" (Isaiah 9:6).

<u>Christ Came From Heaven</u>

When Nicodemus said that he and some of the other Pharisees knew Jesus had come from God (John 3:1-2), he most likely meant they realized God had given Jesus special powers in the same way He had given power to the Old Testament prophets. He almost certainly did not realize that he was speaking a literal truth. Even when Jesus acknowledged His heavenly origins (John 3:13), Nicodemus did not understand and Jesus was angry that Israel's so-called spiritual leaders had such hard hearts they could not grasp His teachings (John 3:10).

In another exchange with the Pharisees, Jesus plainly told them that He was from heaven (John 8:23) but again, they did not understand.

As the last of the Old Testament-like prophets, John the Baptist understood who Jesus was and where He had come from for he had received a special revelation from heaven (John 3:27). He told his followers that like them, he himself was from the earth and taught as one from the earth, but that Jesus taught what He had seen and heard in Heaven, for He was from Heaven (John 3:31-33).

<u>Christ as the Bread of Life</u>

Jesus often spoke of Himself as the "bread of life which came down out of heaven." The people would have understood that Jesus was referring to the manna God sent from heaven to feed the Jews after they fled Egypt, but they probably did not understand that Jesus was referring to Himself as the giver of eternal life.

- *John 6:33* "For the bread of God is that which comes down out of heaven, and gives life to the world."

- *John 6:35* Jesus said to them, "I am the bread of life; he who comes to Me will not hunger, and he who believes in Me will never thirst."
- *John 6:48* "I am the bread of life."
- *John 6:51* "I am the living bread that came down out of heaven; if anyone eats of this bread, he will live forever; and the bread also which I will give for the life of the world is My flesh."

Christ as the Creator

Creation is commonly perceived to be the work of the Father rather than of the Son or the Holy Spirit. When one hears the name "God" or "Jehovah", it is God the Father who comes to mind, as in these verses concerning God as the Creator:

- *Genesis 1:1* "In the beginning, God created the heavens and the earth."
- *Job 38:1, 4* Then the LORD answered Job out of the whirlwind and said…"Where were you when I laid the foundation of the earth?"
- *1 Corinthians 8:6* "…yet for us there is but one God, the Father, from whom are all things and we exist for Him…"

However we find several verses to indicate that Christ was the Creator. Most notable among these is John 1:1-3 which has already been discussed. John succinctly identifies Christ as pre-existent, as the Creator and as God. Consider this additional evidence in the New Testament concerning Christ as the Creator:

- *Colossians 1:16-17* For by Him all things were created, both in the heavens and on earth, visible and invisible, whether thrones or dominions or rulers or authorities – all things have been created through Him and for Him. He is before all things, and in Him all things hold together.
- *Hebrews 1:10* "You LORD in the beginning laid the foundation of the earth, and the heavens are the works of Your hands."

Yet other Scriptures, particularly in the Old Testament, identify the Holy Spirit as the Creator:

- *Genesis 1:2* The earth was formless and void, and the darkness was over the surface of the deep, and the Spirit of God was moving over the surface of the waters.

What conclusion can be reached concerning these verses? That Scripture contains contradictions? No, not at all. The only sound conclusion is that all three persons of the Triune Godhead were actively involved in the creation process, even if their roles were distinct. So while we are able to distinguish between the three persons, we also see that they are linked to one another in the work of creation. The significance of this evidence is to prove that the Father, the Son and the Holy Spirit are equal in their eternality, power, wisdom, omnipotence, omnipresence and omniscience.

<u>Christ as God</u>

Perhaps the clearest and most direct statement Jesus made concerning His deity seen in John 10:30:

"I and the Father are one."

The Jews had just asked Jesus to tell them plainly if He was the Messiah and even after He answered in the most direct manner possible, the hard-hearted Jews accused Him of blasphemy. They refused to believe the miracles they had witnessed with their own eyes and would not believe what Jesus had told them.

Finally, we have no greater evidence than the word of the glorified Christ:

> # "I am the Alpha and the Omega" says the Lord God, "who is and who was and who is to come, the Almighty."
>
> *(Revelation 1:8)*

Scripture has proven that Christ was exactly who He said He was: Creator, Savior, and Almighty God. He has existed from eternity past.

But what did He do? What was His work? This will be the subject of our next lesson.

LESSON 1–SUMMARY

READ

John 14:28, Proverbs 8:22, John 8:58, Exodus 3:14, John 17:5, John 1:1-3, John 17:24, John 1:15, 30, Mark 1:7-8, Ephesians 1:3-4, Micah 5:2, Isaiah 9:6, John 3:1-2, John 3:13, John 3:10, John 8:23, John 3:27, John 3:31-33, John 6:33, John 6:35, John 6:48, John 6:51, Genesis 1:1, Job 38:1, 4, 1 Corinthians 8:6, Colossians 1:16-17, Hebrews 1:10, Genesis 1:2 John 10:30, Revelation 1:8

REFLECT

Why is the doctrine of the eternality of Christ foundational to the Christian faith?

_____

_____

_____

Where can we find evidence that Christ was pre-existent and is eternal?

_____

_____

_____

When Nicodemus said he knew Jesus had come from God, what did he actually mean?

_____

_____

_____

What was the significance of Jesus' statements concerning being the bread of life?

_____

_____

_____

Various verses in Scripture separately identify the Father, the Son and the Holy Spirit as the Creator. Since the Bible contains no errors and no contradictions, how can these verses be explained?

_____

_____

_____

REMEMBER

The doctrine of the eternality of Christ is foundational to the Christian faith because if Christ is not eternal, then no eternal Trinity exists, He cannot be God, He cannot be the Creator and He cannot be our Savior.

The Bible provides all the evidence we need to prove that Christ was pre-existent and is eternal.

Nicodemus probably meant that he and some of the other Pharisees believed God had given power to Jesus like He had given to the Old Testament prophets.

When Jesus spoke of being the bread of life, the people would have remembered how God sent manna from heaven to feed — and save — the Israelites in the desert. In saying that He was the bread of life, Jesus was using an analogy to help the people understand that He was offering to save them and provide eternal life.

Although various Scriptures identify the Father, Son and Holy Spirit individually as the Creator, there are no contradictions because all three, being persons of the Triune Godhead, did in fact participate in the creation process, albeit in different roles.

Seeking Son Light

Section 3
The Life of Christ

Lesson 2
The Angel of the Lord

Every visible manifestation of God in bodily form in the Old Testament is the Son of God, the Second Person of the Trinity.

Section 3: The Life of Christ
Lesson 2: The Angel of the Lord

In the previous lesson, we learned that Jesus Christ was pre-existent and eternal. We know He participated in the process of creation but what happened after that? A great deal of time passed between creation and Bethlehem. What did Jesus do during that time? What were His activities? Did He just go into retirement after Creation?

It comes as a surprise to many that Christ was active on the earth during the Old Testament period. In fact, Scripture makes it clear that His work was a common and continual ministry to God's people. He dealt with sin, provided for those in need, protected God's people from their enemies and in general, executed the will of God.

New students of the Old Testament often believe that Jesus Christ made no appearances during that time. Oh, but He did! He appeared or is mentioned approximately 50 times in the Old Testament. However, He was not known as Jesus at that time; Jesus was His earthly, human name which He received at His birth (Matthew 1:25). In His Old Testament work, the Son of God was typically known as The Angel of the Lord.

Scholars agree it is safe to assume that every visible manifestation of God in bodily form in the Old Testament is the Son of God, the second Person of the Trinity.

The word to describe these Old Testament appearances of Christ is the-ophany *(thee-off-any)*. In the Greek this word is: *theos* (meaning God) and *phaino* (meaning appearing). This is yet more evidence that The Angel of the Lord truly was the pre-incarnate Christ.

He's No Angel

In the previous lesson, several biblical passages were presented as an argument against the Arian beliefs that taught Christ was a created being; in other words, an angel. So how can we reconcile the use of the term "The Angel of the Lord" in connection with Christ?

Used in its Scriptural context, the term "The Angel of the Lord" is more like a job title than a description of the person.

As proven by the Bible verses mentioned in Lesson 1, Christ is eternal and He is God. Angels are created beings.

Also, angels refuse to be worshipped (Revelation 19:10, 22:8-9) acknowl-edging themselves to be fellow servants of God, but The Angel of the Lord accepted the worship of men on at least two occasions (Exodus 3:1-6; Joshua 5:14-15).

There is more evidence to show that The Angel of the Lord was the Second Person of the Trinity:

He claimed to be God: In Exodus 3, we are told that The Angel of the Lord appeared to Moses in the midst of a bush that was burning but was not being consumed. When He identified Himself to Moses He said, "I am the God of Abraham, the God of Isaac and the God of Jacob (Exodus 3:6) and later said His name was "I AM who I AM" (Exodus 3:14). These are claims of deity.

Those who saw Him acknowledged Him as God: Upon seeing The Angel of the Lord, Hagar said, "You are a God who sees" (Genesis 16:7, 13). Gideon knew that he had seen God face to face (Judges 6:22) as did Manoah and his wife (Judges 13:21-22).

The Angel of the Lord promised to do what only God can do: He provided a substitute sacrifice to prevent Abraham from sacrificing Isaac (Genesis 22:11-13).

He told Hagar that she would have too many descendants to count (Genesis 16:10). He comforted her after Abraham sent her away with her son and promised to make him into a great nation (Genesis 21:14-19). He told Moses He had heard Israel's cry and He would deliver them from Egypt (Exodus 3:7-8). We know that these promises came true. Only God could have made and kept those promises.

How can we know that The Angel of the Lord was not God the Father or the Holy Spirit?

The Bible answers that question as well.

- *John 1:18* "No man has seen God at any time; the only begotten God who is in the bosom of the Father, He has explained Him."
- *1 Timothy 6:15-16* "…He who is the blessed and only Sovereign, the King of kings and Lord of lords, who alone possesses immortality and dwells in unapproachable light; whom no man has seen or can see."
- *John 5:37* "And the Father who sent Me, He has testified of Me. You have neither heard His voice at any time, nor seen His form."
- *John 14:17* "(that is) the Spirit of truth, whom the world cannot receive, because it does not see Him or know Him but you know Him because He abides with you, and will be in you."

Appearances of the Angel of the Lord

Many of us have a fixed image of Christ in our minds: a humble preacher walking the dusty paths of Galilee wearing sandals and a long white garment, with a surprisingly well-groomed beard and long wavy hair. A different image emerges when we consider these appearances of The Angel of the Lord.

The Angel of the Lord stood in the road to oppose Balaam and prevent him from traveling to Moab to curse the Israelites. Although Balaam was not able to see The Angel of the Lord at first, his donkey was able to see Him and stopped in her tracks three times. When God opened Balaam's eyes, he saw The Angel of the Lord standing before him with His sword drawn (Numbers 22:22-31).

This warrior with sword drawn was the Second Person of the Trinity who

appeared in the New Testament as the humble preacher that we know as Jesus Christ.

When Moses saw the burning bush, it was The Angel of the Lord who appeared to him in flames (Exodus 3:2).

The Angel of the Lord appeared in a pillar of cloud by day and in a pillar of fire at night to lead the Israelites out of Egypt (Exodus 13:21). He never left His place in front of His people except when Pharaoh's chariots and horsemen came in pursuit of them, and at that time He positioned Himself between Pharaoh's army and His people to protect them (Exodus 14:19-20).

Gideon thought he was simply conversing with a traveler who was holding a staff and sitting under an oak tree near Gideon's property. The traveler used the staff to consume an offering of meat and bread and then disappeared. Gideon realized he had seen The Angel of the Lord face to face (Judges 6:22).

Similar Ministries

As New Testament believers, we have the benefit of hindsight to understand that the ministries of Jesus Christ and The Angel of the Lord were very similar. John Walvrood identifies some of the similarities. "In the Old Testament, The Angel of the Lord is sent by God to reveal truth, to lead Israel and to defend and judge them. In the New Testament, Christ is sent by God the Father to reveal God in the flesh, to reveal truth, and to become the Savior. It is characteristic for the Father to send and the Son to be the sent one."

The Angel of the Lord never appears again after Jesus' birth in Bethlehem. He isn't even mentioned in the pages of the New Testament and this seems strange considering His active ministry in the Old Testament. The best explanation for this disappearance is that The Angel of the Lord, the Son of God, continues His ministry to God's people as Jesus Christ.

Quoting John Walvrood once again: "The important fact which stands out above all others is that the Savior of the Old Testament is the Savior of the New. He was actively engaged in bringing salvation in its widest sense to those who trusted Him."

In the next lesson, we will explore how (and why) the Second Person of the Trinity left behind His very powerful role as The Angel of the Lord to become a helpless babe in Bethlehem.

LESSON 2–SUMMARY

READ

Matthew 1:25, Revelation 19:10, Revelation 22:8-9, Exodus 3:1-6, Joshua 5:14-15, Exodus 3:6, Exodus 3:14, Genesis 16:7, 13, Judges 6:22, Judges 13:21-22, Genesis 22:11-13, Genesis 16:10, Genesis 21:14-19, Exodus 3:7-8, John 1:18, 1 Timothy 6:15-16, John 5:37, John 14:17 Numbers 22:22-31, Exodus 3:2, Exodus 13:21, Exodus 14:19-20, Judges 6:22

REFLECT

What did the Son of God do from the time of Creation until He was born in Bethlehem as Jesus Christ?

_____

_____

_____

When people look in the Old Testament for Jesus Christ, why might they have trouble finding Him?

_____

_____

_____

We know from various Scriptures studied in Lesson 1 that the Second Person of the Trinity (Jesus Christ to us) was not a created being, that is, not an angel. Why is He referred to in the Old Testament as The Angel of the Lord?

_____

_____

_____

How do we know The Angel of the Lord was the Son of God and not God the Father or the Holy Spirit?

_____

_____

_____

How was the ministry of the Son of God in the Old Testament similar to His ministry in the New Testament?

_____

_____

_____

REMEMBER

The Son of God was very active on the earth during the Old Testament period. His work was a common and continual ministry to God's people.

The Son of God was known as The Angel of the Lord during Old Testament times. The name Jesus is His earthly, human name that He received upon His birth in Bethlehem.

The Angel of the Lord as used in the Old Testament is more like a job title than a description of the person. The Son of God is not a created being. He is eternal; He is God.

We know it was the Son of God who appeared as The Angel of the Lord because Scripture tells us that no man has seen God the Father at any time, and that the Holy Spirit is also invisible.

In the Old Testament, The Angel of the Lord is sent by God to reveal truth, to lead Israel and to defend and judge them. In the New Testament,

Christ is sent by God the Father to reveal God in the flesh, to reveal truth and to become the Savior. The Father *sends* and the Son is the One who is *sent*.

Seeking Son Light

Section 3
The Life of Christ

Lesson 3
Miracle in a Manger

We will build a greater understanding of His remarkable life, His awesome love and His unfathomable sacrifice.

Section 3: The Life of Christ
Lesson 3: Miracle in a Manger

There have always been myths surrounding the birth of Jesus Christ. For example, many assume that Mary was about 20 years old when the angel Gabriel appeared to her. In reality, she was much younger. When we think about her journey to Bethlehem to register for the census, we tend to assume she rode a donkey because that is the image we see on Christmas cards. Being poor people, it is unlikely Joseph even owned a donkey and they probably walked the 80 miles from their home in Nazareth. Another typical Christmas scene shows the three wise men standing in the stable at the feet of the newborn Jesus. The truth is the magi did not arrive for days, weeks or even months after His birth.

In this lesson we will discuss the truths surrounding the birth of Jesus and in so doing, we will expose the myths.

> Our goal is to let the *facts* about Christ create the framework upon which we will build a greater understanding of His remarkable life, His awesome love and His unfathomable sacrifice.

We will discuss the roles each of the following people played in the great event of Christ's birth and how they reacted to their situations. How would we react if we were to find ourselves in similar circumstances? Can we see ourselves in any of their responses?

Mary

The Bible tells us little about Mary. Based on what we know about the marriage customs at that time, she was very young, probably no older than 14 when she was visited by the angel Gabriel and given life changing news.

Anytime Scripture describes an encounter between an angelic being and a human, a word that is often used to describe the human's reaction is "fear". Gabriel previously appeared to Daniel and Zechariah, both of whom were gripped by fear (Daniel 8:15-17; Luke 1:11-12). Daniel wrote that he was so frightened, he fell on his face!

Mary was frightened and she was perplexed (Luke 1:26-29), pondering what all of this could mean. Gabriel told her not to be afraid and that she was favored by God (Luke 1:30).

Notice that Scripture *does not* say that Mary was sinless or was chosen by God based on any other virtue she may have possessed.

She was chosen by God simply because He wanted to choose her.

Gabriel told Mary that she would conceive a child who would be great and would be called the Son of God (Luke 1:31-33). It seems from the biblical account that Mary remained calm and was able to comprehend everything the angel was telling her. She asked how she could conceive a child since she was a virgin and Gabriel told her that the Holy Spirit would "overshadow" her (Luke 1:34-35). We do not know if the "over-shadowing" occurred at that specific moment but we do know this was not a sexual event. It was a supernatural event. Mary truly was a virgin when Jesus was born.

The most striking thing about this account is Mary's willingness to give over her life to satisfy the will of God, and seemingly without hesitation. "May it be done to me according to your word" (Luke 1:38). Did she worry that the townspeople would whisper behind her back? Did she wonder how her betrothed, Joseph, would react? She did not say, "You know, this is a really great offer for a girl like me, but it's just not convenient for me right now." Instead, she acknowledged she was a bond slave to the Lord and she was ready to submit to His will. That was remarkable faith.

Joseph

If the Bible tells us little about Mary, it tells us next to nothing about Joseph. We can surmise however that he was a kind and compassionate man who must have cared deeply for Mary. It was completely within his legal rights to divorce her (in the Jewish culture at that time, an engagement was as binding as a marriage). Instead Joseph planned to quietly terminate their engagement and spare her from public disgrace (Matthew 1:19-NIV).

Admittedly, Mary's story about the pregnancy would have been a hard pill to swallow for any man but Joseph was visited in a dream by an angel who reassured him that Mary's story was indeed true (Matthew 1:20-24). Being a godly man, Joseph remained by Mary's side and served as Jesus' protector and human father figure for the rest of his life.

It was not long after Jesus was born that Joseph was called upon to take action to save the baby from men who wanted to kill him. When called to service, Joseph did not wait to see if the warning was true or to reschedule his work to accommodate a trip to Egypt. He immediately got up in the middle of the night and took Mary and Jesus away to safety (Matthew 2:13-14).

Eventually the family returned to their home in Nazareth (Luke 2:39-40). Joseph was a carpenter, a skilled craftsman who passed on the carpentry trade to his son (Mark 6:3). We also know that Joseph raised Jesus in the Jewish traditions and spiritual observances (Luke 2:41).

By all accounts, Joseph was a man of integrity and righteousness.

Through no fault of his own, he found himself in a humiliating situation and yet chose to obey God and be sensitive to someone else's shame. God rewarded Joseph's integrity by entrusting him with the great responsibility of raising His Son.

After the incident with Jesus at the temple when He was twelve years old (Luke 2:41-49), Joseph is never mentioned again in Scripture. The lesson we can learn from him is that we must remain obedient to God even if we are humiliated and disgraced before men.

The Shepherds

What is the significance of the shepherds in the story of Jesus' birth? Sheep herders were not among the elite in society. They were not wealthy and did not have political power. They were simple working people, trying to make a living for themselves and their families.

Of all the people in the world who could have received the birth announcement, God chose to reveal the miracle to the lowly shepherds in the fields. Although at first the shepherds were terrified (Luke 2:9), their terror soon turned to joy when they were told where to find the Messiah. They found Jesus wrapped in cloths lying in a manger just as the angels had told them (Luke 2:12, 16). They were filled with joy as they told everyone the news the angels had revealed to them (Luke 2:17-18, 20).

So what was the shepherds' significance in this story? It is simply that Jesus comes to those with a humble heart and a willingness to accept Him just as He is. Will we be like the shepherds whose joy turned into action, or like the indifferent priests and scribes who were watching for the Messiah but missed Him anyway? That answer can only be found in our hearts.

The Magi

> Magi from the east came to Jerusalem and asked, "Where is the one who has been born king of the Jews? We saw his star in the east and have come to worship him." *(Matthew 2:1-2)*

Matthew is the only gospel writer who tells us the story about the magi. Magi, typically translated "wise men" comes from the Greek *magian*, meaning "astrologer". The magi were thought to have come from a region near Babylon. If that is the case, they would have had access to Old Testament manuscripts that told of a coming Messiah. One such prophecy was spoken by Balaam when he told of a star that would come out of Judah (Numbers 24:17).

The Bible does not say with certainty how many magi came to Jerusalem, but the common belief is that there were three because three gifts are mentioned (Matthew 2:11). However, we are told that when Herod learned of their arrival, he was greatly troubled and all of Jerusalem along with him (Matthew 2:3). Had only three magi arrived, it would have hardly caused a stir in a city the size of Jerusalem. Most likely, there were a great number of people in the caravan that traveled approximately 900 miles seeking the Messiah.

The star led them to the place where the Child was (Matthew 2:9-11). Notice that they were led to a house, not to a stable. How long after Jesus' birth did the wise men arrive? If the star first appeared in the sky on the night of Christ's birth, the magi probably would have seen it and interpreted its meaning within just a few days. It would have taken some time to organize a large caravan to make the 900 mile journey to Bethlehem. Assuming the caravan could travel 20 miles per day, it could have taken them from 15 to 18 months to make the trip.

The Bible does not provide more detailed information about the wise men and their travels. The important lesson to take away from the story of the magi is that they sought the Messiah and left their homes and families to find and worship Him. How can we do less?

Herod

To say that Herod the Great was a tyrant is an understatement. He is sometimes referred to as the "Ruthless King of the Jews" although he was not a Jew at all. He held the position because he was appointed by Rome. His title as ruthless was well deserved. Herod would destroy anything or anyone, including his own family, who challenged his authority and power.

> # Herod's intentions were not as noble as those of the magi who sought only to find and worship the Messiah.

When he discovered the magi's mission, he learned from the chief priests and scribes that the Messiah was to be born in Bethlehem (Matthew 2:6) and he tried to trick the magi into telling him where the child was located (Matthew 2:7-8). Herod said he too wanted to worship the Child but his evil plan was to kill Him.

After finding and worshipping Jesus, the magi were warned in a dream not to reveal Jesus' location to the King so they did not return to Herod (Matthew 2:12). Herod was so enraged that he ordered the slaughter of all male children in the vicinity of Bethlehem who were two years and younger, believing that the infant King of the Jews would be among them (Matthew 2:16). Not long after this incident which is referred to as the Slaughter of the Innocents, Herod died after a painful illness.. Even today, people seek to destroy Jesus Christ but in the process, they only end up destroying themselves. Christ will be victorious.

Oh Holy Night!

We do not know for certain what Bethlehem looked like when Joseph and Mary arrived that night looking for safe and comfortable accommodations. It was a tiny town about six miles south of Jerusalem with a population that barely exceeded 300 people. The town apparently had at least one inn and unfortunately it was full, so in order to put a roof over their heads, Joseph arranged to stay the night in the stable (Luke 2:7). It would have been dark and dirty and smelled of the animals who were sharing the space.

We can imagine details about what happened next, but we can only know for sure what the Bible tells us. We know for certain that a baby boy was born that night. He was wrapped in cloths as was the custom at that time, and placed in a manger, nothing more than a feeding trough.

> # As Mary marveled at her son, she must have been surprised when several shepherds from nearby fields arrived at the stable. *(Luke 2:15-16)*

They said they had been told of the birth by angels who appeared in the sky and told them of the great things this child would accomplish in His lifetime. Did Mary understand the significance of this miraculous event? Probably not. We are told that she pondered these things in her heart (Luke 2:19).

Joseph would have sought better accommodations for his family as soon as possible after the birth. Mary surely needed to regain her strength before beginning the return trip to Nazareth. As a carpenter, perhaps Joseph was able to find work in the town and thus decided to remain in Bethlehem instead of returning to Nazareth at all. We only know that at some point, Joseph moved his family into a house (Matthew 2:11).

Perhaps a year or more later, a large caravan arrived at the house where they were staying and strangers began carrying gifts into the home. They were gifts for the Child and the strangers bowed down to worship Him (Matthew 2:11). Not long after this, Joseph was once again visited in a dream by an angel who told him to get up immediately and flee to Egypt because men would try to kill the Child. He did as he was told and took Mary and Jesus to the relative safety of Egypt (Matthew 2:13-14).

Eventually Joseph and his family returned to Nazareth (Matthew 2:21-23) where Jesus grew into a man and began His public ministry many years later. Every event surrounding Him is miraculous, from His birth in a stable to His resurrection from the dead.

Human Reaction

In this lesson we have discovered the facts and exposed some myths about the birth of Jesus, but what conclusion can we draw?

Mary was little more than a child herself when she was visited by the angel and given life changing news. She agreed without hesitation to submit to the will of God. Joseph was a good man who found himself in a bad situation but after being enlightened by the angel, he too carried out the duty to which he had been called.

The shepherds were filled with wonder and joy at the news that the Messiah had been born and they immediately sought Him out. The magi were watching for the Messiah's sign and upon seeing the star, they left the safety and comfort of their homes to travel a great distance to worship the infant King.

Even though King Herod knew little about Jesus, he was determined to find and destroy Him because in his mind, the infant was a threat to his power and position. The chief priests and scribes were professionally trained to watch for the sign of the Messiah but they missed it anyway. Even when they learned that the magi had traveled 900 miles because they believed the Messiah had been born, they were indifferent and did not make the effort to travel a mere six miles to see for themselves.

The conclusion is that even today, people will have one of these reactions to Christ:

- Like Mary and Joseph, they submit to the will of God. Like the shepherds and magi, they are filled with joy and seek Him out, possibly leaving the comforts of home and family to worship the Savior.
- Like Herod, they hate Him and seek only to destroy Him. In the process, they will only end up destroying themselves.
- Like the chief priests and scribes, they are completely indifferent to Him.

What is your reaction to Christ?

LESSON 3 – SUMMARY

READ

Daniel 8:15-17, Luke 1:11-12, Luke 1:26-29, Luke 1:30, Luke 1:31-33, Luke 1:34-35, Luke 1:38, Matthew 1:19 (NIV), Matthew 1:20-24, Matthew 2:13-14, Luke 2:39-40, Mark 6:3, Luke 2:41, Luke 2:41-49, Luke 2:9, Luke 2:12, 16, Luke 2:17-18, Matthew 2:1-2, Numbers 24:17, Matthew 2:11, Matthew 2:3, Matthew 2:9-11, Matthew 2:6, Matthew 2:7-8, Matthew 2:12, Matthew 2:16, Luke 2:7, Luke 2:15-16, Luke 2:19, Matthew 2:13-14, Matthew 2:21-23

REFLECT

What are some common misconceptions about Mary?

_____

_____

_____

How can we know that Joseph was a kind and compassionate man?

_____

_____

_____

Why are the shepherds included in the story of Jesus' birth?

_____

_____

_____

How might the magi have known that the star represented the Messiah?

_____

_____

_____

Why did Herod want to destroy Jesus?

_____

_____

_____

What are some different reactions people today have concerning Christ?

_____

_____

_____

REMEMBER

People today tend to assume that Mary was around 20 years old when she was visited by the angel Gabriel. It is more likely that she was much younger, probably no more than 14. God did not choose Mary because she was sinless or because of any other virtue she may have possessed. The Bible simply says God favored Mary.

Joseph did not want Mary to suffer public disgrace and he was sensitive to her shame. He planned to quietly divorce her until an angel confirmed that Mary was pregnant by the Holy Spirit. Joseph was a man of integrity and God rewarded him by giving him responsibility for raising His son.

The shepherds were common and humble people. They were not among the elite and did not have any political power. Christ comes to those with a humble heart.

It is believed that the magi came from a region near Babylon. If so, they would have had access to Old Testament manuscripts that foretold of the coming Messiah.

Herod was a ruthless ruler who tried to destroy anyone and anything that challenged his power and position. He did not understand that Jesus' kingdom was not of this earth but was a spiritual kingdom.

Some people react like Mary and Joseph by choosing to accept the will of God. Many are like the shepherds and are joyful when they learn about Jesus. Others are willing to leave home and family like the magi just to worship the Savior. Still others want only to destroy Jesus but ultimately end up only destroying themselves. And far too many are like the chief priests and scribes and are totally indifferent to Christ's coming.

Your reaction to Christ will ultimately determine your eternal destination.

Seeking Son Light

Section 3

The Life of Christ

Lesson 4

The Baptism and Temptation of Christ

Satan may have thought that by being born as a human, Christ would have received the same sinful nature we are born with. He was wrong.

Section 3: The Life of Christ
Lesson 4: The Baptism and Temptation of Jesus

It is not uncommon these days to hear preachers and televangelists use flattery and charm to draw us in to whatever gospel they are preaching. They are often impeccably dressed and highly educated. They promise riches and happiness. There is seldom a mention of sin or the need for repentance. After all, why break the spell that has their audience smiling and attentive? Why rock the boat and risk having empty seats next week? Why deliver a downer of a message by telling them they have a high risk of going to hell?

These charlatans would run and hide from a preacher like John the Baptist. He delivered his harsh message straight up because that is what the people needed to hear. Like the Old Testament prophets that came before him, even his appearance affirmed that he was not about to water down the message he had been sent to deliver.

John was the son of the priest Zacharias and his wife Elizabeth. This elderly couple was childless until they became the recipients of a miracle from God (Luke 1:5-16). As foretold by an angel of the Lord, John, in the spirit and power of Elijah, would be the forerunner before the Messiah (Luke 1:17).

Jewish Baptism

Baptism was common among the Jews in the time of John the Baptist. This cleansing in water was a ceremonial purification and it included not only the people themselves but clothing, utensils and articles of furniture (Leviticus 8:6; Exodus 19:10-14; Mark 7:3-4; Hebrews 9:10).

Clearly, John's baptism was not Christian but it wasn't exactly Jewish either.

John's was a baptism of repentance. His message was that the Messiah was coming soon and time was running out for the people to repent of their sins and change their lives and the baptism itself was an outward sign of their repentance.

John openly acknowledged that he was not the Messiah. He preached that while he baptized with water, the Messiah would baptize with the Holy Spirit and with fire (Matthew 3:11). However, like other Old Testament prophets, John probably did not realize that a significant amount of time would pass between the first baptism and the second, when judgment would come by unquenchable fire.

The Baptism of Jesus

If John's baptism was for repentance, why did Jesus come to be baptized?

It had been revealed to John that the one upon whom the Spirit descended and remained was the One who would baptize in the Holy Spirit (John 1:33-34). When the Holy Spirit descended on Jesus immediately after He came up out of the water, it was John's confirmation that Jesus was indeed the awaited Messiah.

But even before the immersion, it seems that John knew Jesus was different.

When John tried to prevent Jesus from being baptized, Jesus said, "Permit it at this time; for in this way it is fitting for us to fulfill all righteousness" (Matthew 3:13-15). What did Jesus mean by this statement?

In "An Exposition of the Gospel of Matthew", Allen Ross conducts an analysis of the word "righteousness". What is intrinsically "right" has to be in harmony with the will of God. God's will for Christ had been laid out in Scripture for centuries. Isaiah said that the suffering servant would be numbered with the transgressors (Isaiah 53:12). Here He began to be identified with sinners. Isaiah further states that the suffering servant was the Righteous One, God's Servant, and would justify many (Isaiah 53:11). Ross continues:

"So the Messiah, the Servant of the LORD in Isaiah, would identify with sinners, take their sins on Himself, and justify them through the suffering He would endure. Jesus was saying that this baptism was the beginning of all that; it was here that He began to fulfill the righteous will of God that He become the Suffering Servant who would take on Himself the sins of the world. This baptism was the inauguration of that ministry."

When Jesus came up out of the water, the voice of God was heard saying, "This is My beloved Son in whom I am well pleased" (Matthew 3:16-17). This expressed His approval of Christ's commitment to perform the whole will of God.

Jesus in the Wilderness

Immediately after His baptism, Jesus was led by the Holy Spirit into the wilderness where He was tempted by Satan for forty days (Mark 1:12-13). Mark consolidates the entire event into these two verses while both Matthew and Luke provide greater detail (Matthew 4:1-11; Luke 4:1-13).

What was the point of this exercise? Before answering that question, consider the use of the word *temptation*. It can be understood in two different ways:

- Temptation is a solicitation to sin. It is an effort to cause a person to sin; to do that which is contrary to God's will. Satan's temptations always fall into this category.
- The word translated as "temptation" can also be translated as "test". In such cases, it is an opportunity for one to be proven righteous. This is God's point of view concerning temptation. It is an opportunity to deepen one's faith.

Jesus is God so why did Satan think he could corrupt Jesus and entice Him to sin?

Satan may have thought that by being born as a human, Christ would have received the same sinful nature we are born with. He was wrong.

Even though Jesus is fully man, He is also fully God. Christ does not have and never has had, a sinful nature. So although Satan put temptations before Christ like he puts them before us, Christ did not sin because it is not in His nature to sin (Matthew 4:1; Hebrews 2:18, 4:15; James 1:13). He is incapable of sin.

So again we ask the question: If Jesus *could not* sin, what was the point of this exercise?

The main reason the Holy Spirit led Jesus Christ into the wilderness to face Satan's challenges was to prove that He was qualified to complete the mission to which He had been called; that is, to serve as the instrument of God's plan for the redemption of mankind. The forty days Jesus spent in the wilderness gave Satan a chance to hit Him with his best shot because Satan wanted nothing more than to divert Jesus from His mission. If Jesus had given in to Satan's temptations, He would never have made it to the cross and we would be lost.

Let's consider the three temptations that are described in the Gospels.

- Turn stone into bread to satisfy His hunger.
- Jump off the highest pinnacle of the temple to see if God would save Him.
- Take the fast track to owning all the kingdoms of the world by falling down to worship the devil.

Notice that all three of these temptations are unique to One who is divine. A mere man cannot be tempted to turn stone into bread because that is something only God can do. A mere man might jump off a tower believing God will save him, but he would most likely discover God's brand of salvation involves the death of the body. And trying to own all the kingdoms of the world is not a realistic goal for any human being.

Satan obviously and deliberately attacked Christ. How did Christ respond?

In response to each temptation, Christ took up the sword of the Spirit which is the Word of God (Ephesians 6:17) to repel Satan's attacks. Matthew is a master of understatement when he says, "After He had fasted forty days and forty nights, He then became hungry" (Matthew 4:2). Christ was undoubtedly hungry and exhausted. Satan intentionally waited until Christ was possibly at His weakest and most vulnerable point to hit Him with the first temptation: turn stones into bread. But Jesus immediately fired back from the Word of God:

> ## "...It is written, Man shall not live on bread alone but on every word that proceeds out of the mouth of God."
> *(Deuteronomy 8:3)*

When Satan suggested that Jesus throw Himself down from the pinnacle of the temple, he quoted two verses from Psalm 91 (Psalm 91:11-12). (By the way, Satan took these verses out of context in order to make them fit this particular situation). Jesus countered by quoting Deuteronomy 6:16:

> ## "You shall not put the Lord Your God to the test..."

Satan finally offered to give Jesus Christ all the kingdoms of the world if only He would bow down and worship him. But of course, Jesus was prepared with Scripture to counter this attack:

"You shall fear only the Lord Your God and you shall worship Him and swear by His name." *(Deuteronomy 6:13)*

And when the devil had finished every temptation, he left Him until an opportune time (Luke 4:13).

<u>What the Temptations Teach Us about Satan</u>

The temptations of Christ give us the opportunity to learn about our adversary, Satan. While Satan crafted temptations unique to Christ, we know that he uses the same methods and techniques against us, although our temptations are often more subtle and indirect. Satan has an ally inside each one of us: what Scripture calls our *flesh*. That is one reason the Holy Spirit indwells each believer; that is to help combat our own sinful desires.

What have we learned about Satan?

- <u>He attacks us when we are at our weakest and most vulnerable point</u>. As human beings, we become exhausted, sad, discouraged, distracted, stressed, worried and anxious. The fast pace of modern life often leaves little or no time for the Bible, but the Word of God is the only source of peace in this dangerous and evil world. When we ignore God's Word, we are missing the opportunity to build a stockpile of ammunition for use against the devil.
- <u>Satan knows Scripture very well</u>, even though he misquotes and misuses it to make it fit whatever need he has at the moment. The

only way we can fight against him is to be aware of his schemes and to gain as great an understanding of Scripture as we can.

- <u>Satan never stops attacking us</u>. He even goes directly to God to point out our weaknesses and failures to Him. Fortunately, Christ is like our defense attorney by interceding on our behalf with God. (Romans 8:34)

What the Temptations Teach Us about Christ

We have already established the fact that Jesus could not have sinned. And by facing these temptations, He proved once and for all that He was worthy to complete the task to which He had been called.

What else have we learned?

- <u>The very same weapon used by Jesus against Satan is available to us</u>. It is the Word of God. For each challenge Satan posed, Jesus fired back with truths from Scripture. Understanding Scripture is the only way we can build up and stockpile ammunition to fight temptation.
- <u>A person's spiritual condition is more important than his phys-ical condition.</u> It would have been impossible for Jesus to preach self-denial if He had succumbed to the temptation to satisfy His own physical hunger by turning stones into bread. But He with-stood the temptation. He also tells us not to fear those who can kill the body but cannot kill the soul (Matthew 10:28).
- <u>Temptation in and of itself is not a sin</u>. It is when we act upon that temptation that sin has occurred. Satan's temptations are God's tests. Satan wants us to sin but when we use the Word of God to

resist him and his temptations, it helps to deepen our faith and strengthen our understanding.

- <u>Jesus knows what it is like to be tempted but not what it is like to sin</u>. It was not possible for Jesus to sin because He does not have a sinful nature. But He understands how Satan comes to us and tempts us when we are at our weakest and most vulnerable point. He will help us through the temptations and provide a way out for us (1 Corinthians 10:13).

LESSON 4 – SUMMARY

READ

Luke 1:5-16, Luke 1:17, Leviticus 8:6, Exodus 19:10-14, Mark 7:3-4, Hebrews 9:10, Matthew 3:11, John 1:33-34, Matthew 3:13-15, Isaiah 53:12, Isaiah 53:11, Matthew 3:16-17, Mark 1:12-13, Matthew 4:1-11, Luke 4:1-13, Matthew 4:1, Hebrews 2:18, Hebrews 4:15, James 1:13, Ephesians 6:17, Matthew 4:2, Deuteronomy 8:3, Psalm 91:11-12, Deuteronomy 6:16, Deuteronomy 6:13, Luke 4:13, Romans 8:34, Matthew 10:28, 1 Corinthians 10:13

REFLECT

How was traditional Jewish baptism different from John the Baptist's baptism?

_____

_____

_____

Why did Jesus come to John to be baptized?

_____

_____

_____

What are two ways *temptation* can be understood?

_____

_____

_____

Why did Satan tempt Christ?

_____

_____

_____

Could Christ have sinned? Why or why not?

_____

_____

_____

What weapon did Christ use to resist Satan's attacks?

_____

_____

_____

What are some things we learned about Satan by studying Christ's temptations?

_____

_____

_____

What are some things we learned about Christ by studying His temptations?

_____

_____

_____

REMEMBER

Traditional Jewish baptism was simply a ceremonial washing. It had nothing to do with repentance or righteousness. John preached that the people had little time to repent because the Messiah was coming soon.

He urged them to repent of their sins and to be baptized as an outward sign of that repentance.

Jesus came to John to be baptized not because He needed to repent of any sins but to "fulfill all righteousness". The baptism was the inauguration of Christ's ministry.

The word temptation can be understood either as a solicitation to sin or as a test from God. Satan's intent is to cause a person to sin and to do that which is contrary to God's will. God's intent is to use that temptation as a test to prove one's righteousness and to deepen one's faith.

Through the temptations, Satan hoped that Christ would disqualify Himself from being able to accomplish His mission; that is, to be God's instrument for His plan for the redemption of mankind. But Christ did not sin and proved once and for all that He was fully qualified to fulfill the task He had been given.

Scripture teaches that Christ could not have sinned. He does not have a sinful nature like we have and He was incapable of sinning. So while He knows what it is like to be tempted, He does not know what it is like to sin.

Jesus used the Word of God to repel Satan's attacks. Satan also used Scripture but he used it out of context and tried to make it fit his own purposes. But Christ could not be deceived. We need to make sure we have a clear understanding of Scripture so Satan cannot deceive us.

We learned that Satan attacks us when we are at our weakest and most vulnerable. He knows Scripture very well but he misquotes and misuses it. He cannot be trusted. Also, Satan never stops attacking us. He even goes directly to God to point out our weaknesses and failures.

By studying the temptations of Christ, we learned that He is perfectly qualified to be the instrument of God's plan for redemption of mankind. The very same weapon He used against Satan is available to us; that is, the Word of God. We also learned that a person's spiritual condition is more important than his physical condition. Temptation in and of itself is not a sin. It is when we act upon the temptation that we fall into sin.

Seeking Son Light

Section 3

The Life of Christ

Lesson 5

An Overview of Jesus' Ministry

News about Him spread all over Syria and large crowds from Galilee, the Decapolis, Jerusalem, Judea and the region across the Jordan followed Him.

Section 3: The Life of Christ
Lesson 5: An Overview of Jesus' Ministry

A person starting his own business today is encouraged to develop a mission statement for his enterprise. According to *Entrepreneur Magazine*, a mission statement is a key tool that is as important as a business plan. It states in just a few sentences the essence of the company's goals and philosophies. In short, it describes what the company is all about.

Jesus was in the business of salvation. If He had agreed with the notion that He needed to develop a mission statement, Luke 4:18-19 reveals what it would have been:

> ## "The Spirit of the Lord is upon Me, because He anointed Me to preach the gospel to the poor. He has sent Me to proclaim release to the captives, and recovery of sight to the blind, to set free those who are oppressed, to proclaim the favorable year of the Lord."

Unfortunately, the people in Nazareth to whom He made the statement did not understand Him. They were offended and filled with rage and they tried to throw Him off a cliff (Luke 4:28-29).

Why did Jesus come to earth? The question is easy enough; it's the answer that gets tough. Here are just some of the correct answers:

- Jesus came to reveal the Father (Matthew 11:27).
- He came to save sinners (1 Timothy 1:15).
- He came to fulfill prophecy (Romans 15:8).
- He came to serve (Mark 10:45).
- He came to provide a pattern for holy living (1 Peter 2:21).
- He came to destroy the works of the devil (1 John 3:8).
- He came to preach (Luke 4:43).
- He came that men might have life more abundant (John 10:10).
- He came to bear witness to the truth (John 18:37).

Jesus accomplished all of these things and the depth to which His life can be studied in regard to His mission is endless. However the focus of this study will be Christ's ministry from a human perspective. We will consider His interaction with His disciples, the Jewish leaders and those whom He came to save.

The Ministry Begins

It is generally accepted that the baptism of Jesus marked the official beginning of His ministry. Matthew, Mark and Luke each write that after Jesus was tempted in the wilderness for forty days, He went up to Galilee and began teaching there (Matthew 4:12; Mark 1:14; Luke 4:14). However a careful reading of John's gospel reveals that Jesus spent a few months in Judea before beginning His Galilean ministry. Some scholars estimate Jesus spent between three and five months in Judea during that portion of His ministry. Among the events which occurred during that time were the first cleansing of the temple (John 2:13-16), the night time visit of Nicodemus (John 3:1-21) and turning water into wine at Cana (John 2:1-11).

The Pharisees began to notice that Jesus was gaining popularity among the people, so He left the area for Galilee knowing the time had not yet come for a public confrontation with the Jewish leaders (John 4:1-3).

The Galilean Ministry

When Jesus arrived in Galilee, He preached and performed miracles (Mark 1:14). He also recruited the twelve apostles who then began traveling with Him throughout the region. Jesus concentrated the greatest part of His ministry in Galilee, spending perhaps as much as 18 months in that region. He had come to present Himself as the Messiah to the Jewish people and Galilee had the single largest concentration of Jews in all of Israel. These were the common people and they were more likely to be receptive to Jesus' offer of salvation which required genuine repentance.

The people of Galilee were considered by the leaders in Judea to be unsophisticated and impious. Although Galilee had more Jews than Judea, more Gentiles lived there as well. Perhaps this is why the Galileans were not as strict in observing the traditions of the elders and the Judeans had little but contempt for them.

During His Galilean ministry, Jesus made His headquarters in Capernaum (Matthew 4:13), a small fishing village with a population of around 1,500 located on the northern shore of the Sea of Galilee. Capernaum was a garrison town, housing a detachment of Roman soldiers under a centurion, along with administrative officials. Unlike Nazareth, which was located in a mountainous region and was somewhat isolated, Capernaum was on a major international trade route and travelers bound for Europe, Asia and Africa regularly passed through the area. Matthew tells us that news about Jesus spread throughout the entire region:

News about Him spread all over Syria and…large crowds from Galilee, the Decapolis, Jerusalem, Judea and the region across the Jordan followed Him.

(Matthew 4:24-25)

It is no wonder that news about Jesus traveled so quickly. During His Galilean ministry, He must have performed literally hundreds of miracles, most of which were healing. These miracles were intended to authenticate His ministry so people would understand that He had been sent from God. But many people seemed to view Jesus as somewhat of an entertainer. He was doing something new and different and people wanted to see what He would do next. Their eyes witnessed the miracles but they did not see; their ears listened to the message that the Kingdom of God was near, but they did not hear. They saw the Messiah they had been waiting for but did not recognize Him and let Him go.

Although Jesus' headquarters were in Capernaum, He traveled throughout Galilee at least three times. The purpose of these preaching tours was to ensure that He carried His message to every village in the region.

Many familiar sermons, teachings and healings occurred during the Galilean ministry and are described in the Gospels. The Sermon on the Mount was conducted during this time and the parables were told. The following is a list of just some of the events that occurred during this period:

- Jesus teaches in the synagogue in Nazareth (Luke 4:16)
- Healing of a demon-possessed man (Mark 1:21-26)

- Healing crowds in Capernaum (Luke 4:40-41)
- Jesus heals a leper (Matthew 8:1-4)
- Jesus heals at the Sea of Galilee (Mark 3:7-12)
- Jesus chooses the Twelve (Mark 3:13-19)
- Jesus preaches the Sermon on the Mount (Matthew 5:1 – 7:29)
- Jesus explains why He teaches in parables (Matthew 13:10-17)
- Jesus calms the storm (Luke 8:22-25)

In spite of His preaching, teaching and healing in Capernaum and the surrounding towns, they did not listen to Jesus' message and refused to repent. As a result, Jesus strongly rebuked them (Matthew 11:20-24) and He left the area.

The Perean Ministry

The name Perea is not found in the Scriptures but it was the term used by the historian Josephus and others for the section of territory east of the Jordan River. In the Gospels, this area is frequently referred to as "the land beyond the Jordan". John the Baptist ministered in that area and was martyred there at Herod's fortress of Machaerus. This land today is in the Arab Kingdom of Jordan.

Because threats had been made against Him, Jesus went to Perea to avoid further confrontation with the Jewish and political leaders (John 11:53-54). He remained in the area for several months ministering to the people in the land across the Jordan and preparing His disciples for what was to come.

Although Matthew, Mark and John mention some events that occurred during this time, the main source of information concerning the Perean ministry is found in the book of Luke.

Much of Jesus' teaching during this period concerned the cost of discipleship and the morality demanded for entrance into the Kingdom:

- Jesus teaches about the narrow way (Luke 13:22-30)
- Jesus teaches about humility (Luke 14:7-14)
- The cost of following Jesus (Luke 14:25-35)
- Jesus teaches about faith and service (Luke 17:1-10)
- Jesus and the rich young ruler (Luke 18:18-27)

The Judean Ministry

Jesus' Judean ministry began with the Feast of Tabernacles approximately six months before His final Passover. After telling His brothers that He was not going to the Feast, He later decided to go in secret (John 7:8-10).

Some of the events that occurred during this period were:

- Traveling to Jerusalem, Jesus heals ten lepers in Samaria (Luke 17:11-19)
- Jesus forgives a woman caught in adultery (John 8:1-11)
- Jesus visits Martha and Mary in Bethany (Luke 10:38-42)
- Jesus raised Lazarus from the dead (John 11:1-44)
- Jesus makes His triumphal entry into Jerusalem (Matthew 21:1-11)

However, first and foremost among the events that occurred during the Judean ministry was the growing conflict between Jesus and the Jewish leaders. The conflict had existed throughout Jesus' public ministry. What issues were in dispute?

- Jesus' interpretation of God's Law (Matthew 5:20) concerning, among other things, activities on the Sabbath (Matthew 12:1-2), fasting (Mark 2:18-22), ceremonial cleansing (Matthew 15:1-3) and caring for aging parents (Matthew 15:4-9).
- He refused to answer their questions about His authority to forgive sins (Mark 11:27-33).
- The Jewish leaders accused Jesus of blasphemy (John 10:31-33).
- Jesus cleansed the Temple of the money changers (Matthew 21:12).

When Jesus began His public ministry, word about Him spread quickly throughout the entire region, including Jerusalem. People were amazed at Jesus' teaching and the miracles He performed. As mentioned earlier, Capernaum was on a major international trade route and travelers carried news of Him wherever they went.

The Jewish leaders were immediately skeptical of Jesus. After all, He was not the first to claim to be the Messiah. But they soon discovered that Jesus was different from those who had come before. He performed miracles and taught with authority. It appeared that He was finding favor with many of the people and the leaders knew they were in danger of losing their comfortable and prestigious lives.

The priests and scribes were highly respected and they had great political power and wealth. They had made themselves indispensible to the people by creating rules and regulations which only they were qualified to interpret. The leaders placed greater importance on these man-made rules than on God's Word and Jesus was teaching the people what the Scriptures *really* said. Consequently they felt threatened by Jesus and they conspired to kill Him.

As Jesus continued to preach in and around Jerusalem the leaders increased their efforts to trap Him and put Him to death. The conflict continued to grow until the leaders were able to find an ally among Jesus' followers: Judas Iscariot. With the help of this betrayer, the Jewish leaders were able to put their evil plan into motion.

Right up to the last day of His life, Jesus continued to prepare His apostles for His death and what lay beyond. This will be the subject of our next lesson.

LESSON 5–SUMMARY

READ

Luke 4:18-19, Luke 4:28-29, Matthew 11:27, 1 Timothy 1:15, Romans 15:8, Mark 10:45, 1 Peter 2:21, 1 John 3:8, Luke 4:43, John 10:10, John 18:37, Matthew 4:12, Mark 1:14, Luke 4:14, John 2:13-16, John 3:1-21, John 2:1-11, John 4:1-3, Mark 1:14, Matthew 4:13, Matthew 4:24-25, Luke 4:16, Mark 1:21-26, Luke 4:40-41, Matthew 8:1-4, Mark 3:7-12, Mark 3:13-19, Matthew 5:1 – 7:29, Matthew 13:10-17, Luke 8:22-25, Matthew 11:20-24, John 11:53-54, Luke 13:22-30, Luke 14:7-14, Luke 14:25-35, Luke 17:1-10, Luke 18:18-27, John 7:8-10, Luke 17:11-19, John 8:1-11, Luke 10:38-42, John 11:1-44, Matthew 21:1-11, Matthew 5:20 , Matthew 12:1-2, Mark 2:18-22, Matthew 15:1-3, Matthew 15:4-9, Mark 11:27-33, John 10:31-33, Matthew 21:12

REFLECT

What are just some of the reasons Jesus Christ came to the earth?

_____

_____

_____

Why did Jesus spend so much time in Galilee?

_____

_____

_____

How did news of Jesus' teaching and miracles spread so quickly throughout that entire region?

_____

_____

_____

How do the Scriptures refer to the land of Perea?

_____

_____

_____

What were some of the things Jesus disputed with the Pharisees?

_____

_____

_____

REMEMBER

Jesus came to earth to reveal the Father and bear witness to the truth. He came to save sinners and to fulfill prophecy. Jesus provided a pattern for holy living for us to follow and He came that we all might have life more abundant.

Jesus had come to present Himself as the Messiah to the Jewish people and Galilee had the single largest concentration of Jews in all of Israel. Also, these were common people and they were more likely to be receptive to Him.

The city of Capernaum was located on a major international trade route and travelers regularly passed through the area. When the travelers heard about Jesus' miracles, they took news of Him wherever they went.

In Scripture, when a reference is made to "the land beyond the Jordan" it is referring to the land of Perea.

Jesus knew the Pharisees were hypocrites and they were burdening the people with needless man-made rules and regulations. Some of the things Jesus disputed with the Pharisees were their rules and regulations for observance of the Sabbath, fasting and ceremonial washing. The Pharisees had also developed a way for the people to get around having to take care of aging parents which was contrary to the teachings of Moses. The priests and scribes knew that Jesus threatened their comfortable lives, wealth and power. They were determined to put down the threat by killing Jesus.

Seeking Son Light

Section 3
The Life of Christ

Lesson 6
The Last Supper

To be seen as great in the eyes of God,
we must be seen as less in the eyes
of men.

Section 3: The Life of Christ
Lesson 6: The Last Supper

The previous lesson presented an overview of Jesus' three-year public ministry which officially began with His baptism. He spent nearly half of that time touring Galilee and ministering to the people there. Several months were spent in the Perea, or "the land beyond the Jordan" and the final portion of Jesus' ministry was spent in Judea.

The final week of His life is sometimes referred to as Passion Week. *Passion* is taken from the Greek word meaning "to suffer" and that is an appropriate description of what Jesus experienced during that time.

Passion Week began with Jesus' triumphal entry into Jerusalem (Luke 19:28-38). A great crowd went out to meet Him as He rode a young donkey into the city and the people praised Him (John 12:12-15). Only a few days later, the people cried out for Jesus to be crucified (Matthew 27:22-23).

Jesus at the Temple

The Jewish leaders allowed people to purchase animals for sacrifices from dealers who set up shop in the temple area. However, the people were required to pay for the animals in money that was acceptable to the priests, meaning they had to exchange their own currency for "temple" currency. The money changers were men who exchanged the currency and charged exorbitant fees.

Jesus' first order of business when He arrived at the temple was to cleanse it of those who would turn it into a den of robbers (Matthew 21:12-13). The animal dealers and money changers were using the temple for personal profit with no consideration for the sanctity of God's house.

> # And He was teaching daily in the temple; but the chief priests and the scribes and the leading men among the people were trying to destroy Him. *(Luke 19:47)*

Many of the people had witnessed Jesus raise Lazarus from the dead just a few days earlier and they were telling others of His miracles. The Pharisees were very angry that the people were following Jesus and they sent spies out into the crowds to try to catch Him in an offense that would allow them to arrest Him (Luke 20:20) but they were unable to do so. When Jesus began to teach in parables that were directed at the Pharisees (Luke 20:19) and put them in an especially bad light, they tried even harder to find a way to arrest and kill Him. Much to their delight, Judas Iscariot chose to become their ally (Luke 22:3-6).

Preparing for the Passover

Passover is an annual celebration commemorating the release of the Jews from bondage in Egypt. God gave Moses very specific instructions concerning how the Passover was to be observed (Exodus 12:1-13) and the celebration has been conducted in that manner throughout the generations.

Passover fell during Passion Week and certain arrangements had to be made for Jesus and the Twelve to share the Passover feast. Jesus told Peter and John how to locate the room in which they could share the meal (Luke 22:10). Although Jesus' instructions were somewhat vague, Peter and John found everything exactly as He had told them (Luke 22:11-13).

The Last Supper

Leonardo De Vinci may have been a great painter but his depiction of the Last Supper in terms of the participants' posture and even the furniture was off the mark. It was common for the participants to recline (Mark 14:18) on sofa-like seating at a U-shaped table. The table was open in the middle for the servants to bring food. It was not the custom for all of the guests to be seated in chairs on one side of a long banquet table as shown in the painting.

The "Last Supper" as is it now known, ratified this new covenant and anticipated the end of the old covenant, although of course no one but Jesus knew this at the time. And it was far from being a joyful event as sometimes portrayed by artists. It was a time of great confusion, fear and sadness.

Several events occurred during the evening and we cannot know for certain in which order they took place. However, some scholars believe the events unfolded in this order: (1) a dispute among the disciples (Luke 22:24), (2) Jesus washed the disciples' feet (John 13:5), (3) Jesus announced that He would be betrayed (Matthew 26:21), and (4) Jesus instituted the Lord's Supper (Luke 22:19-20).

This is the order in which we will study the events.

A Dispute Among the Disciples

All of the preparations had been made, and Jesus and the other disciples arrived at the upper room (Mark 14:17). A dispute arose among the disciples concerning who would be the greatest in the new kingdom (Luke 22:24-27). Now, these were the men who had spent three years learning from Jesus. They had received information from Jesus about His kingdom that no one else in the world had received, and yet after all this time they still did not understand. Remember, at this point they had not yet received the Holy Spirit; they had not been born again and they were spiritually dead.

> # Their hopes and aspirations were defined by their worldly desires, and no one in this world aspires to be a servant.

Aware of their conversation, Jesus used the opportunity to demonstrate how an act of humility can convey the deepest level of love.

A Lesson in Humility

It was the custom in those days for a servant to wash a guest's feet upon their arrival at the home. Most people wore open sandals and their feet became very dusty and dirty. This act of hospitality was performed by the lowliest servant and was certainly never performed by the master of the house. Knowing this, the disciples were taken aback when Jesus poured water into a basin and began to wash their feet (John 13:5). Peter was indignant, at first refusing to allow Jesus to wash his feet but he relented when Jesus insisted on performing this act (John 13:8-9). Jesus was teaching them a lesson in humility and service (John 13:12-17).

By example, Jesus taught the disciples that to be seen as great in the eyes of God, they had to be seen as less in the eyes of men.

A Betrayer Among Us

As they were reclining at the table, Jesus revealed that one of them would betray Him that very night (John 13:21-22). One must wonder if there was a collective gasp in the room. These men were like brothers. They surely thought they knew one another well enough to spot a traitor in their midst.

We do not know for certain why Judas betrayed Jesus but there have been many theories. One possibility is that he did it strictly for the money, having received thirty pieces of silver to help trap Jesus. Another theory is that Judas had become disillusioned with Jesus and believed He had failed the nation. Whatever the reason, Judas became a willing participant in the events that ultimately allowed God's plan to come to fruition.

John seems to give us special insight into these events (John 13:23-30). Apparently John, the beloved disciple, was sitting very close to Jesus when He made the statement about the betrayal. From across the table, Peter caught John's eye and gestured to him to ask Jesus who the traitor was. When Jesus answered that it was the one to whom He would give the morsel, was that for John's ears only? That appears to be the case. We are told that the other disciples did not know why Judas left the room or where he was going. They believed that Jesus had apparently sent him on some special mission.

Do This in Remembrance of Me

> And when He had taken some bread and given thanks, He broke it and gave it to them saying, "This is My body which is given for you; do this in remembrance of Me." And in the same way He took the cup after they had eaten, saying, "This cup which is poured out for you is the new covenant in My blood." *(Luke 22:19-21)*

And with these words and actions, Christ instituted the observance variously known as Communion, the Lord's Supper and the Eucharist.

The disciples who were present at the Last Supper did not understand the significance of the event at the time and the synoptic gospels only provide very brief summaries. The occasion of the gathering was to celebrate the Passover but the portion of the celebration that is told in the Gospels is totally foreign to the Passover ritual. John, who writes his Gospel decades later, does not even record the event but instead includes Jesus' extensive teaching on that evening, which has come to be known as the Upper Room Discourse (John 13-17). Jesus did not attempt to explain to the disciples all that He was doing, knowing they could not understand its significance until His work on the cross was finished.

Although there are differing beliefs among Christians concerning the deeper theological meaning of the Lord's Supper, most conservative evangelical Christians believe that this observance is a *symbolic memorial* that serves to remind us of Christ's sacrifice. By participating in the observance, we acknowledge that we are Christians and that we have been reconciled to God through Christ's shed blood. Like the baptism service, it is a public declaration that we have been raised to life in Christ.

Although the confines of this lesson do not permit an in depth study of the other theological beliefs concerning the Lord's Supper, they are identified below for any who wish to do further independent study:

Transubstantiation – The Roman Catholic and Eastern Orthodox belief that the Eucharistic elements become the body and blood of Christ while keeping only the appearance of bread and wine.

Consubstantiation – Martin Luther's teaching that the fundamental "substance" of the body and blood of Christ are present alongside the substance of the bread and wine, which remain present.

Real Presence – John Calvin's view insists on the real, though spiritual presence of the Lord in the Supper. This view teaches that the believer *actually receives*, not figuratively or metaphorically, but *actually receives* Christ's body and blood in the Supper. The Holy Spirit unites Christ's body and blood with the elements even though Christ's body is in heaven at the right hand of God.

After singing a hymn, they went out to the Mount of Olives. *(Mark 14:26)*

And with that, the group left the upper room and headed for the Garden of Gethsemane where Jesus knew He would be arrested. Jesus had less than 24 hours to live. His march to the cross had begun.

LESSON 6 – SUMMARY

READ

Luke 19:28-38, John 12:12-15, Matthew 27:22-23, Matthew 21:12-13, Luke 19:47, Luke 20:20, Luke 20:19, Luke 22:3-6, Exodus 12:1-13, Luke 22:10, Luke 22:11-13, Mark 14:18, Luke 22:24, John 13:5, Matthew 26:21, Luke 22:19-20, Mark 14:17, Luke 22:24-27, John 13:8-9, John 13:12-17, John 13:21-22, John 13:23-30, Luke 22:19-21, John 13-17, Mark 14:26

REFLECT

Who were the money changers and why was Jesus opposed to them?

_____

_____

_____

Why were the Pharisees angry about the parables Jesus told at the temple? What did they try to do?

_____

_____

_____

What did Jesus know about the Last Supper that the disciples did not know?

_____

_____

_____

What lesson did Jesus want the disciples to learn when He washed their feet?

_____

_____

_____

What is the conservative evangelical view of the Lord's Supper and what does it say about those who participate in it?

_____

_____

_____

REMEMBER

The temple leaders allowed people to purchase animals for sacrifice, but payment had to be made in money that was acceptable to the priests. The money changers exchanged the currency at exorbitant fees. It was inappropriate for any of these activities to take place on the temple grounds and was an affront to the sanctity of God's house.

The parables Jesus told as He taught at the temple came a little too close to home for the Pharisees because the stories made them look bad. They sent spies out into the crowd to try to catch Jesus in some offense so He could be arrested, but they were unable to do so.

The Last Supper, also known as the Lord's Supper, ratified the new covenant and anticipated the end of the old covenant, but Jesus was the only person who knew this at the time. The new covenant would be ushered in when His work on the cross was finished.

By washing the disciples' feet, Jesus wanted them to learn that to be seen as great in the eyes of God, they had to be seen as less in the eyes of men.

Most conservative evangelical Christians believe the Lord's Supper is a symbolic memorial that serves to remind us of Christ's sacrifice. By participating in the observance, we acknowledge that we are Christians and that we have been reconciled to God through Christ's shed blood.

Seeking Son Light

Section 3

The Life of Christ

Lesson 7

The Arrest and Trial of Jesus

We see Christ's humanity in the Garden
of Gethsemane.

Section 3: The Life of Christ
Lesson 7: The Arrest and Trial of Jesus

We see Christ's humanity in the Garden of Gethsemane. Having studied His life to this point, we have seen Jesus adored by His followers, feared by the demons, loved by His disciples and hated by the Jewish leaders. Jesus has always had the upper hand, has always been in control and has always had the last word in the verbal sparring matches with the Pharisees.

Now we see Jesus with His face to the ground, in agony over His approaching death. His sweat was like drops of blood falling to the ground (Luke 22:44) and He was overwhelmed with sorrow to the point of death (Matthew 26:38).

How can we understand the enormity of His agony? Christ was agonizing over more than the physical pain associated with the beating and crucifixion; His pain was even deeper than that. He was facing separation from God as He alone carried the unfathomable burden of human sin. Jesus Christ, the sinless Son of Man bore the full measure of His Father's wrath to satisfy His righteous anger so men could have peace with God.

Agony in the Garden

Just a short time earlier, Jesus and the disciples sang a hymn (Mark 14:26) and left the upper room, going out to the Garden of Gethsemane which was at the foot of the Mount of Olives. It was a beautiful and serene location where Jesus often met with the disciples (John 18:2).

Judas was well aware of the location and Jesus had no intention of going into hiding.

As they approached the garden, Jesus instructed the disciples to keep watch with Him and to pray they would not fall into temptation (Luke 22:40). What kind of temptation were they in danger of falling into? Perhaps they would be tempted to try to prevent Jesus' arrest. They might be tempted to resist God's will for Jesus and for themselves rather than submit to it. Or they might be tempted to believe that Jesus was not the Messiah after all and He had simply deceived them. Jesus knew there were difficult times ahead for the disciples and only prayer would provide the strength they needed to persevere. Peter, John and James went into the garden with Jesus and as He urged them to continue to pray, Jesus left them and went further into the garden alone.

"My Father, if it is possible, may this cup be taken from me. Yet not as I will, but as you will." *(Matthew 26:39)*

What was this "cup" that Jesus spoke of?

- *For a cup is in the hand of the Lord…surely all the wicked of the earth must drain and drink down its dregs (Psalm 75:8).*
- *For thus the Lord, the God of Israel, says to me, "Take this cup of the wine of wrath from my hand and cause all the nations to whom I send you to drink it." (Jeremiah 25:15).*
- *Rouse yourself! Rouse yourself! Arise, O Jerusalem, you who have drunk from the Lord's hand the cup of His anger; the chalice of reeling you have drained to the dregs (Isaiah 51:17).*

- *If anyone worships the beast and his image, and receives a mark on his forehead or on his hand, he also will drink of the wine of the wrath of God which is mixed in full strength in the cup of His anger...(Revelation 14:9-10).*

The cup that Jesus asked to be taken away was the cup of God's wrath. The "cup" was foretold in the Old Testament and it is still present in the Book of Revelation. It is the cup that is deserved by all mankind and that will be poured out on unbelievers in the future. Those who believe that Christ accepted the cup on their behalf will be spared.

As Jesus prayed He returned three different times to the disciples who were also to be praying and keeping watch with Him. But each time He returned to them, He found them sleeping. Luke tells us they were exhausted from sorrow (Luke 22:45). These are the same men who, only hours earlier vowed to die for Him if necessary. And even though He urged them to pray, Jesus found them sleeping instead (Matthew 26:45).

Now an angel from heaven appeared to Him, strengthening Him. And being in agony He was praying very fervently; and His sweat became like drops of blood, falling down upon the ground.

(Luke 22:43-44)

We already know that Jesus had prayed for the "cup" to be taken from Him. Did this angel come to give Him the answer to that prayer? Did the angel say, "Sorry Jesus, but Your Father is still going with Plan A. You will be abused and beaten, mocked and spit at. Then You will hang on the cross until You die." Jesus would hardly have been spiritually strengthened by a message like that.

Luke, being a medical doctor, knew that the enormous spiritual and emotional strain Jesus was under would manifest itself in His physical condition. He has already told us that the disciples were exhausted from sorrow (Luke 22:45). The disciples actually had very little information at that time and yet their physical response was exhaustion: they were physically spent. How much more severe was Jesus' physical response considering the knowledge He possessed? Luke tells us that Jesus' sweat was like drops of blood falling to the ground and Mark says He was grieved to the point of death (Mark 14:34).

Physically, Jesus was *literally* at the point of death. One scholar has suggested that without the physical sustenance brought by the angel from heaven, Jesus might actually have died in the Garden of Gethsemane. The word for "strengthened" is used in one more place in the New Testament, where Paul was said to have been "strengthened" by taking some food after a three day fast (Acts 9:19). It is clear that the word refers to a physical strengthening. It also reminds us that the angels came to minister to Jesus after His 40 days in the wilderness (Matthew 4:11; Mark 1:13). Thus, after being strengthened by the angel, Jesus prayed even more fervently.

The Arrest

The temple leaders' evil plan, devised with the assistance of Judas, was now in motion. As Jesus was speaking to the disciples, Judas appeared accompanied by a large crowd carrying swords and clubs (Matthew 26:47). While we are not told exactly how many people came to arrest

Jesus, John makes reference to the "Roman cohort" (John 18:12). A *cohort* is a detachment of soldiers numbering 600.

The signal Judas used to identify Jesus was a kiss on His cheek, but this did not come as a surprise to Jesus (Luke 22:48). As soon as the identification was made, the soldiers moved in to arrest Jesus. In Philippians 2:10, Paul tells us

> ...at the name of Jesus, every knee will bow of those who are in heaven and on earth and under the earth...

Keeping this in mind, we now turn to the gospel of John.

> So when He said to them, "I am He", they drew back and fell to the ground.
>
> *(John 18:6)*

This large crowd of people was seeking an insignificant itinerate preacher from Nazareth but what they found was One who publically declared His exalted and divine identity. The power of Jesus' majesty was too great for them and they fell to the ground.

Paul does not say that every knee will bow *voluntarily*, only that every knee *will* bow to Jesus. Those who came to arrest Jesus were seeing a picture of what awaits all of mankind. He is the Lord and Master who will demand recognition and worship.

The Trial of Jesus

Several years ago, the Honorable Harry Fogle, a judge and member of the Jurisdictionary Foundation, Inc. did a study of the Jewish and Roman legal systems that were in place during the time of Jesus. His goal was to determine whether laws had been broken during Jesus' arrest and trial. Judge Fogle wrote from the perspective of a judge and not as a theologian.

His analysis showed that the arrest and trial of Jesus violated the laws of both Israel and Rome. He concludes by saying, "Two of the most enlightened systems of law that ever existed were prostituted to destroy the most innocent man who ever lived." (Read Judge Fogle's entire article, *The Trial of Jesus*, by contacting the Jurisdictionary Foundation, Inc. Public Legal Education, www.jurisdictionary.com)

The Men Who Tried Jesus

Jesus was questioned by several different men before He was condemned.

Annas – The former high priest and patriarch of a very powerful and influential family. At least five of his sons had previously served as high priest and Caiaphas was his son-in-law. He questioned Jesus about His teachings and His disciples but was unable to obtain any information he could use against Him (John 18:13, 19).

Caiaphas – The current high priest and chief judge of the Sanhedrin. It was Caiaphas who had said earlier that it was better for one man to die than for the entire nation to perish (John 11:49-50).

The Great Sanhedrin –This high council was made up of seventy elders, priests and scribes. It dealt with religious and criminal matters but it did not have the authority to impose capital punishment (John 18:31-32). These men were to have impeccable reputations because they served as both judge and jury in the cases it heard. After hearing some false testimony against Jesus (Mark 14:57) they all condemned Him to death (Mark 14:64). Then some of these men with impeccable reputations began to spit at Jesus, blindfold Him and strike Him with their fists (Mark 14:65).

Pontius Pilate – The Roman governor of Judea who had the power to impose the death penalty. Pilate had a stormy relationship with the Jews which in the past had resulted in riots and chaos. Pilate did not believe Jesus was guilty of any crime, certainly not a crime worthy of death, and was reluctant to pass judgment. When he learned that Jesus was a Galilean, he told the priests to take Him to Herod Antipas (Luke 23:6-7).

Herod Antipas – The Roman tetrarch of the region of Galilee and Perea. He did not live in Jerusalem but was in the city at this time because it was Passover season. Herod had heard of Jesus and seemed to have a genuine interest in meeting Him although we do not know his motives. Herod questioned Jesus but He refused to answer. Since Jesus would not amuse him, Herod did not render a decision on the case and sent Him back to Pilate after giving Him a robe fit for a king (Luke 23:8-11).

Pilate, thinking he had neatly disposed of this particular Jewish problem must have been surprised and frustrated when the priests returned with Jesus.

Three different times Pilate declared to the priests that Jesus was not guilty but they persisted. He could not understand what offense Jesus could have committed that had caused these priests to be adamant about His execution. Pilate reminded them that he had the power to release a prisoner of their choosing (Matthew 27:15-18, 20-26), hoping they would choose to release this obviously innocent man. But instead they chose to release Barabbas, a convicted murderer (Luke 23:19).

The priests then reminded Pilate that Jesus had claimed to be a king, and the emperor surely would not look favorably upon Pilate for refusing to eliminate such a rebel. As a result of this thinly veiled threat, Pilate relented to the demands of the priests and condemned Jesus to death, and placed Jesus into the hands of the brutal Roman soldiers (John 19:16).

LESSON 7–SUMMARY

READ

Luke 22:44, Matthew 26:38, Mark 14:26, John 18:2, Luke 22:40, Matthew 26:39, Psalm 75:8, Jeremiah 25:15, Isaiah 51:17, Revelation 14:9-10, Luke 22:45, Matthew 26:45, Luke 22:43-44, Mark 14:34, Acts 9:19, Matthew 4:11, Mark 1:13, Matthew 26:47, John 18:12, Luke 22:48, Philippians 2:10, John 18:6, John 18:13, 19, John 11:49-50, John 18:31-32, Mark 14:57, Mark 14:64, Mark 14:65, Luke 23:6-7, Luke 23:8-11, Matthew 27:15-18, Matthew 27:20-26, Luke 23:19, John 19:16

REFLECT

Jesus told the disciples to pray they would not fall into temptation. What kind of temptation were they in danger of falling into?

_____

_____

_____

What was the "cup" Jesus asked His Father to take from Him?

_____

_____

_____

What type of strengthening did the angel from heaven provide to Jesus?

_____

_____

_____

When the large crowd of people came to arrest Jesus, they experienced something that awaits all unbelievers in the future. What was it?

_____

_____

_____

How many times did Pilate declare Jesus to be innocent? Why did he finally agree to send Jesus for crucifixion?

_____

_____

_____

REMEMBER

The disciples were in danger of being tempted to prevent Jesus' arrest and to resist God's will not only for Jesus but for themselves as well. They were also in danger of being tempted to believe that Jesus was not the Messiah after all and He had simply deceived them.

The cup that Jesus asked to be taken away was the cup of God's wrath. The cup was foretold in the Old Testament and it is still present in the Book of Revelation. It is the cup that is deserved by all mankind and that will be poured out on unbelievers in the future. Those who believe that Christ accepted the cup on their behalf will be spared.

The angel from heaven strengthened Jesus physically. Jesus had told the disciples that He was grieved to the point of death. Some scholars believe that if Jesus had not received this physical strengthening from the angel, He might have actually died before accomplishing His mission.

When Jesus identified Himself to the large crowd that had come to arrest Him, He said, "I AM He". Upon hearing these words, everyone in the crowd fell to the ground. In Philippians, Paul said that "at the name of Jesus, every knee will bow". He did not say that every knee would bow *voluntarily*, as the people in the crowd discovered. Everyone will bow to Jesus as Lord and Master one day.

Pilate declared three times that Jesus was innocent. He finally agreed to send Him for crucifixion when the priests reminded Him that the emperor would not look favorably on one who had refused to eliminate a rebel claiming to be a king.

Seeking Son Light

Section 3
The Life of Christ

Lesson 8
The Crucifixion

His appearance was disfigured beyond
that of any human being and His form
marred beyond any human likeness.

Section 3: The Life of Christ
Lesson 8: The Crucifixion

Although he strongly believed that Jesus was innocent, Pilate was more concerned with his own security than he was with an itinerant preacher from Galilee (John 19:12). He caved under pressure from the priests and turned Jesus over to the Roman soldiers.

What happens next is barely mentioned in the Gospels: Jesus is scourged. Matthew and Mark each devote six verses to the events that occurred between Pilate's condemnation and the cross (Matthew 27:27-31; Mark 15:16-21). John simply states in a single verse, "Pilate then took Jesus and scourged Him" (John 19:1) and Luke makes no mention of it at all.

Jesus is Scourged

When a man was scourged, he was stripped naked, bent over a low post or stump and his hands and feet were chained so he could not move. The beating was done with an instrument called a *flagrum, scourge or flail*. It was a specially designed whip with several long leather straps attached to a handle. Sewn onto the straps were sharp bits of bone, metal and glass. The soldier stood about six feet away from the prisoner, brought the whip back and then thrust it forward with great force. It whistled through the air until it hit its mark, striking the prisoner against the back of his rib cage. The long leather straps curled around the body, the bits of bone and metal tearing the flesh, leaving open and bleeding wounds and exposing muscle and bone.

If the prisoner passed out from the pain, he was splashed with buckets of salt water until he was revived, and then the torture continued. Pain was layered upon pain.

The book of Deuteronomy says that if a man goes to court and is found guilty, and if the crime is deserving of a beating, then he could be struck no more than 40 times (Deuteronomy 25:3). Later the Jews actually changed the maximum number of strikes to 39. In the event the soldier administering the beating lost count, he would not be in violation of God's law.

But Jesus was turned over to the Roman soldiers and unfortunately they did not have a limit on the number of strikes that could be administered. They would bring a man as close to death as they could without actually killing him. They were masters at this form of torture. But even after the scourging, the soldiers were not yet finished with Jesus.

The Roman Soldiers Mock and Beat Jesus

Then the soldiers of the governor took Jesus into the Praetorium and gathered the whole Roman cohort around Him.
(Matthew 27:27)

The soldiers placed a crown of thorns on His head, and dressed Him in a scarlet robe. They gave Him a reed as a staff and knelt before Him, mocking His claims to be a king. They spat on Him and beat Him on the head with the staff. They may have even pulled out His beard.

I gave My back to those who strike Me, and My cheeks to those who pluck out the beard; I did not cover My face from humiliation and spitting. *(Isaiah 50:6)*

The crown of thorns was made from thick vines with thorns that are up to three inches long. If Jesus was wearing this "crown" while the soldiers beat Him on the head, the thorns would have been driven into His scalp and forehead causing severe bleeding.

Beaten, bruised, and bleeding, Jesus was then taken away to be crucified.

...there were many who were appalled at Him–His appearance was so disfigured beyond that of any human being and His form marred beyond any human likeness–*(Isaiah 52:14, NIV)*

<u>The Art of Crucifixion</u>

It is believed that the Persians invented crucifixion in the fourth century B.C. as a means of capital punishment. But it was the Romans who perfected it. The Romans wanted to inflict as much pain as possible for as long as possible before death. Their objective was to create a form of punishment that could be done in public and would provide a real deterrent to crime and rebellion. They found crucifixion to be more effective in this regard than death by spear, boiling in oil, impalement, drowning or burning people alive.

When a prisoner was crucified, he carried his own crossbeam to the execution site. He was made to lie on the ground with his arms outstretched over the crossbeam. Long iron nails were driven through the prisoner's wrists to hold him onto the beam. It is believed that straps may have also been used to help support the prisoner's weight to prevent death from coming too soon.

The crossbeam was then lifted onto an upright post that stood about seven feet high. The cross probably looked like a capital "T". There was often a small seat called a *sedulum* which helped support the prisoner's weight. The knees were bent and rotated laterally in order for the feet to be nailed to the post.

Crucifixion was actually death by slow suffocation. With arms fixed in an outstretched position it was very difficult for the prisoner to exhale and it was impossible for him to take a full breath. As time slowly passed, the prisoner would experience severe muscle cramps and contractions. The shallowness of breathing caused small areas of the lungs to collapse. Due to the shallow breathing, the body could not expel the carbon dioxide. Fluid built up in the lungs; the heart was stressed and eventually failed.

It is Finished

The execution site was less than one-half mile from the fortress where Jesus was scourged, but after His severe beating at the hands of the Roman soldiers, Jesus was too weak to carry the 80 to 100 pound crossbeam. A man from Cyrene who had come to Jerusalem for the Passover was enlisted to carry the crossbeam for Him (Luke 23:26).

In Hebrew, the name of the execution site was "Golgatha", meaning "the Place of the Skull" (John 19:17) so named because some said the rock formations and caves made the place look like a human skull. The Latin name for the execution site was Calvary.

Jesus was nailed to the cross at 9:00 on Friday morning. A sign was raised above His head showing the charge against Him:

The King of the Jews *(Mark 15:26)*

The soldiers were allowed to keep the clothing of their victims and they cast lots to divide up Jesus' garments between them (Matthew 27:35), fulfilling David's prophecy:

They divide my garments among them and cast lots for my clothing. *(Psalm 22:18)*

As Jesus hung on the cross, the chief priests, elders and scribes came to mock Him (Matthew 27:41). They must have felt a sense of victory and satisfaction as they watched Jesus suffer, knowing they had put down the rebel who had challenged them. Even the robbers who were being crucified along with Him threw insults at Him (Matthew 27:44).

I am poured out like water, and all My bones are out of joint. My heart has turned to wax; it has melted away within Me. My strength is dried up like a potsherd, and My tongue sticks to the

roof of My mouth; you lay Me in the
dust of death. *(Psalm 22:14-15)*

For dogs have surrounded Me; a band
of evildoers has encompassed Me.
They pierced My hands and My feet;
I can count all My bones. They look;
they stare at Me. *(Psalm 22:16-17)*

From the sixth hour to the ninth hour (from noon until 3:00 p.m.) darkness came over all the land (Mark 15:33) and surely those who had participated in the plot against Jesus must have wondered at it. It was as if nature itself was in mourning for Christ.

At about the ninth hour (3:00 in the afternoon), Jesus cried out:

"Eloi, Eloi, lama sabachthani? Which
means, "My God, my God, why have
you forsaken me?" *(Matthew 27:46)*

Isaiah tells us that sin separates us from God.

But your iniquities have separated you
from your God; your sins have hidden
His face from you, so that He will not
hear. *(Isaiah 59:2)*

Having taken all of mankind's sins upon Himself, Jesus knew that God had turned His face away from Him. *This* is the cup that Jesus asked to be taken away from Him. The physical agony is unfathomable and nearly impossible to describe. But it was this spiritual separation from God that Jesus dreaded. He suffered double death so we would never have to experience separation from God.

<blockquote>
… Jesus said, "It is finished!" With that, He bowed His head and gave up His spirit. *(John 19:30)*
</blockquote>

LESSON 8–SUMMARY

READ

John 19:12, Matthew 27:27-31, Mark 15:16-21, John 19:1, Deuteronomy 25:3, Matthew 27:27, Isaiah 50:6, Isaiah 52:14(NIV), Luke 23:26, John 19:17, Mark 15:26, Matthew 27:35, Psalm 22:18, Matthew 27:41, Matthew 27:44, Psalm 22:14-15, Psalm 22:16-17, Mark 15:33, Matthew 27:46, Isaiah 59:2, John 19:30

REFLECT

What does Deuteronomy 25:3 say about flogging?

_____

_____

_____

Describe the Roman practice of scourging.

_____

_____

_____

What do the prophecies in the book of Isaiah tell us about the treatment Jesus received at the hands of the Roman soldiers?

_____

_____

_____

In the Garden of Gethsemane, Jesus prayed that the "cup" be taken from Him. What was it specifically about the "cup" that Jesus dreaded so much?

_____

_____

_____

How do believers benefit from the Jesus' suffering?

_____

_____

_____

REMEMBER

The number of times a man could be struck during a flogging was specified in Deuteronomy 25:3. It stated that a man could not be struck more than 40 times. The Pharisees later changed the number to 39 so if the soldier administering the blows lost count, he would not be in violation of God's law.

The Roman practice of scourging was designed to bring a prisoner as close to death as possible without actually killing him. They used a specially designed whip with bits of bone, metal and glass sewn into the leather straps in order to inflict great pain and to cut into the prisoner's skin and muscles. If a prisoner passed out from pain during the scourging, he was splashed with buckets of salt water until he was revived and then the beating continued.

The great suffering that Jesus underwent at the hands of the Romans was described centuries before in the book of Isaiah. One prophecy stated that Jesus would give His back to His torturers and would even withstand the pain of having His beard pulled out by the soldiers. Another prophecy says His beating was so severe that He was barely recognizable as a human being and those watching were appalled at His appearance.

We know from an earlier lesson that the "cup" Jesus asked to be taken away from Him was the cup of God's wrath. For Jesus, that meant spiritual separation from God. Although the agony of the physical torture is nearly impossible to describe, it was the separation from God that Jesus dreaded most. He suffered a "double death"; that is He died both physically and spiritually.

Because Jesus willingly took the cup of God's wrath and suffered both physical and spiritual death and separation from God, believers do not have to endure this suffering themselves. Although all humans will experience physical death, they need not suffer spiritual death and separation from God because of the work Jesus accomplished on the cross.

Seeking Son Light

Section 3
The Life of Christ

Lesson 9
The Resurrection

He has risen!

Section 3: The Life of Christ
Lesson 9: The Burial and Resurrection

The priests had won. Jesus' lifeless body was hanging on the cross waiting to be disposed of. They would no longer have to deal with this insignificant preacher from Nazareth. As Jesus Himself had said, "It is finished."

Christ had been crucified by the Romans (albeit at the insistence of the Jews) and it was Roman practice to allow the bodies of those crucified to hang on the cross until they decayed. Ancient writings refer to "feeding crows on the cross". However it was the Jewish custom to bury the dead; they even buried their enemies. Typically the dead would be buried in the family "plot" but the Jews would not permit the bodies of executed criminals to be placed in family tombs where they might desecrate those already buried. Instead they provided a burial site for criminals just outside the city, a Jewish version of "boot hill" as described in stories about the American Old West.

> ## His grave was assigned with wicked men, yet He was with a rich man in His death. *(Isaiah 53:9)*

Jesus had been executed as a criminal. He was executed with criminals. And based on Jewish custom, He would be buried with criminals as well. What could change the course of the events already in motion to fulfill Isaiah's prophecy about the suffering servant's burial?

Everything concerning the death of Jesus Christ was done in a rush. The Jews would have preferred to wait until the Passover celebration was over to arrest and execute Jesus, but they were given an unexpected opportunity at the hand of Judas Iscariot. Once Jesus was in their custody, they had to rush through the trial in order to get Him to Pilate in time for the death sentence to be carried out that day. This process was delayed somewhat when Pilate sent Jesus to Herod, but Herod returned Jesus to Pilate and they were back on track again. Once the death sentence was pronounced and carried out, the Jews were in a rush for the condemned men, including Jesus, to die so the bodies could be taken down and buried before 6:00 P.M. when the Sabbath officially began.

Jesus died around 3:00 in the afternoon and His death was confirmed when a Roman soldier stabbed a spear into His side. The two thieves who were crucified with Jesus were still alive at that time so in order to hasten their death, the soldiers crushed the bones in their legs with a heavy piece of lumber. This method was typically used when the condemned lingered too long on the cross (John 19:31-34).

He keeps all His bones; Not one of them is broken. *(Psalm 34:20)*

No one in Jesus' family dared to ask for His body and it appeared that He was destined for burial in "boot hill."

Apparently unbeknownst to Jesus' family and followers, a prominent member of the Sanhedrin went to Pilate to ask permission to take Jesus' body for burial (Mark 15:43). The Roman governor was under no obligation whatsoever to grant the request and the fact that he did so was less about making amends for condemning an innocent man to death than it was about antagonizing the Jewish priests. Whatever Pilate's motives, he released Jesus' body to Joseph of Arimathea.

Luke tells us that Joseph was a secret follower of Jesus and that he had not consented to the Council's plans to crucify Him (Luke 23:50-51). We have already been told of another member of the Sanhedrin named Nicodemus who, while perhaps not yet a true follower of Jesus, did appear to be a genuine seeker of truth (John 3:1-2). Now we see these two men working together to prepare Jesus' body for burial (John 19:38-41). Perhaps realizing they could not stop the Sanhedrin's plan to crucify Jesus, the two men may have made plans in advance to at least provide Him with a proper burial. Nicodemus obviously required some amount of time to purchase the nearly 100 pounds of spices and Joseph would have needed time to obtain the clean linen cloth.

It does not appear however that Joseph had planned in advance to bury Jesus in the tomb he had prepared for himself, but because time was quickly running out, they decided to place Him there (John 19:42).

And although this good and righteous man did not realize it, God used him to fulfill a prophecy.

Showing their belief and respect for Jesus in this way was no small sacrifice for Joseph and Nicodemus. When the Council moved forward with its plan to crucify Jesus, they both verbally expressed their disapproval. But by actually taking charge of the body, preparing it for burial and then placing it in Joseph's own tomb, both Joseph and Nicodemus were crossing a line. When they went to take Jesus off the cross, it is very likely that at least some members of the Council were still at the crucifixion site where they would have observed the actions of these two men. Joseph and Nicodemus could have been forced out of the Sanhedrin, lost their livelihoods, their status and possibly their families.

It is also interesting to note that the women were apparently unaware that Jesus' body had already been prepared with spices before being laid in the tomb. John's Gospel does not say that the women were present at the burial, but Matthew, Mark and Luke all indicate that the women waited to see where the body was placed (Matthew 27:61; Mark 15:47; Luke 23:55). Either the women did realize that Jesus' body had already been prepared with spices or they did not trust the two men to do it right. In any case, they planned to return to the grave after the Sabbath to anoint Jesus' body themselves.

Sabbath Day

Never had the disciples seen such a dark day.

They were overcome with grief, regret, fear, uncertainty, despair, and confusion.

Grief because they had loved Jesus and now He was gone; regret because like cowards, they had run away and were unable to save Him; fear because they believed the authorities were coming for them next; uncertainty because they had left their old lives behind to follow Jesus and now they had nothing; despair because they had no hope for the future; and confusion because they had truly believed Jesus was the Messiah. How could they have been so wrong? Only two days ago, they had discussed which among them would be the greatest in the new kingdom. Now that hope was not only dashed, it was totally crushed.

The Bible provides no details concerning the location of the disciples on the Sabbath day. The common belief is that they returned to the "upper room" where earlier they had shared the Passover meal with Jesus. They apparently shared this space with many other followers of Jesus, including the women who planned to return to the tomb on the following day to anoint His body. They knew this loving gesture was the last thing they could do for Him now. They would prepare the spices and leave for the tomb before dawn.

Meanwhile, Back At the Temple…

Unlike the disciples, the chief priests had not forgotten that Jesus said He would rise again in three days (Matthew 16:21). They went to Pilate, asking that he seal the tomb and place guards there (Matthew 27:62-66). This would prevent the disciples from stealing the body in an attempt to claim that Jesus had indeed risen from the dead.

The priests thought they were in complete control of the situation.

They knew where Jesus' body had been placed. They knew He had claimed to rise again. The priests convinced Pilate they would be worse off than before if His disciples came to steal the body. The tomb was sealed and soldiers from the world's best fighting force were stationed at the entrance. There was no way anyone was going to get inside that tomb.

While it was within their power to keep the disciples from going *into* the tomb, they could not stop Jesus from coming *out* of the tomb. And sadly, even these prestigious and highly respected men who served as Israel's teachers of the Scriptures, did not even consider it a possibility.

The Empty Tomb

In today's chaotic world, it is not unusual to have our regular programming interrupted because of a major breaking news story. As the reporters strive to be the first to go on the air with the story, sometimes information gets reported as fact that later turns out to be fiction. The bigger the story, the more confusion abounds. Only after all of the facts have been confirmed or denied do we get a complete and accurate picture of the event.

Regardless of discrepancies in the minor details, the occurrence of the central event cannot be denied.

Such was the case in the discovery of the empty tomb as reported in the Gospels. We get a real sense of the excitement and confusion of that morning as the women reported the events to the disciples.

Matthew reports that two women went to the tomb. An earthquake had occurred. The stone had been rolled away and an angel sat upon it. Jesus appeared to both women and sent a message to the disciples. The guards were terrified and fainted. The priests later bribed them to keep them quiet and promised to intercede with the Roman governor if necessary (Matthew 28:1-15).

Mark writes that three women went to the tomb and when they arrived, the stone had already been moved away from the entrance. The saw an angel sitting inside the tomb and he told them Jesus had risen from the dead. Jesus appeared but apparently only Mary Magdalene saw Him. Mark mentions neither the earthquake nor the reaction of the guards (Mark 16:1-11).

Luke tells that an unnamed number of women went to the tomb and they discovered that the stone had already been moved. Two angels appeared and stood near them. In Luke's account, Jesus does not appear to the women and there is no mention of the earthquake or of the guards (Luke 24:1-12).

John says that Mary Magdalene went to the tomb alone. The stone had already been moved away from the entrance when she arrived and she immediately ran back to tell Peter and John that Jesus' body had been removed. John writes that Mary Magdalene apparently went to the tomb again later and at that time, she saw two angels sitting inside where the body of Jesus had been lying. She turned around and saw Jesus who spoke to her and gave her a message for the disciples (John 20:1-18).

Remember that the writer of each Gospel reported events from his own perspective. Matthew wrote that two women went to the tomb. Perhaps he was unaware that other women went along as well. Mark writes that Jesus appeared to two women, but John chose to report that Jesus appeared only to Mary Magdalene. In the Gospel accounts, we see that each writer chose to include or emphasize certain events as they pertained to his own audience. These differences in no way imply contradictions. In fact, the details in each of the Gospels can be linked together to create a consistent, stand-alone account of the resurrection.

The following account was taken from the book, *The Case for the Resurrection of Jesus* by Gary Habermas:

- Jesus is buried; several women watch *(Matthew 27: 61; Mark 15: 47; Luke 23:55)*.
- The tomb is sealed and a guard is set *(Matthew 27:62-66)*.
- At least three women, including Mary Magdalene, Mary the mother of James, and Salome, prepare spices to go to the tomb *(Matthew 28:1; Mark 16:1)*.
- An angel descends from heaven, rolls the stone away, and sits on it. There is an earthquake and the guards faint *(Matthew 28:2-4)*.
- The women arrive at the tomb and find it empty. Mary Magdalene leaves the other women there and runs to tell the disciples *(John 20:1-2)*.
- The women still at the tomb see two angels who tell them that Jesus has risen and instruct them to tell the disciples to go to Galilee *(Matthew 28:5-7; Mark 16:2-8; Luke 24:1-8)*.
- The women leave to bring the news to the disciples *(Matthew 28:8)*.
- The guards, having roused themselves, report the empty tomb to the authorities, who bribe the guards to say the body was stolen *(Matthew 28:11-15)*.
- Mary the mother of James and the other women, on their way to find the disciples, see Jesus *(Matthew 28:9-10)*.
- The women relate to the disciples what they have seen and heard *(Luke 24:9-11)*.
- Peter and John run to the tomb, see that it is empty, and find the grave clothes *(Luke 24:12; John 20:2-10)*.
- Mary Magdalene returns to the tomb. She sees the angels and then she sees Jesus *(John 20:11-18)*.

Also, the most important evidence that the Gospel accounts are true is that all of them agree that the tomb was empty and that Jesus had risen from the dead.

- "He is not here, for He has risen, just as He said." (Matthew 28:6)
- "He has risen; He is not here; behold, here is the place where they laid Him." (Mark 16:6)
- "He is not here, but He has risen." (Luke 24:6)
- For as yet they did not understand the Scripture, that He must rise again from the dead. (John 20:9)

Forty Days on Earth

Something drastic happened to the apostles between Thursday night when they ran away from the Garden of Gethsemane and Sunday morning when they discovered the empty tomb.

John indicates that on Sunday morning, they still did not fully understand the Scriptures (John 20:9). They knew the tomb was empty and they knew they had not taken Jesus' body. The Jewish leaders certainly would not have taken it. After all, they had asked Pilate to place guards at the tomb to be certain no one took it.

And then Jesus appeared. Their fear and despair were replaced by joy (John 20:20). And Jesus was with them for forty days, teaching them how all the Scriptures had pointed to Him, from Moses to the prophets (Luke 24:45). He prepared them to go out and make disciples of all the nations (Mark 16:16-20).

During these forty days, Jesus showed His followers that He was truly alive. He spoke with them, walked with them and ate with them. By the end of those forty days, many questions had been answered for the apostles.

One of the most convincing proofs of Christ's resurrection is the change in the apostles themselves.

After receiving the Holy Spirit, they were transformed from men who ran away from trouble, even to the point of denying they even knew Jesus, to strong and fearless apostles who willingly submitted to jail, beatings and even death, for the sake of Jesus Christ and His message.

We too are transformed when we place our trust in Jesus Christ. We receive the Holy Spirit, the Comforter and Counselor, to teach us and help us live for Christ. This is a transformation that continues from the moment we accept Christ until we meet Him in Heaven and share His glory.

LESSON 9–SUMMARY

READ

Isaiah 53:9, John 19:31-34, Psalm 34:20, Mark 15:43, Luke 23:50-51, John 3:1-2, John 19:38-41, John 19:42, Matthew 27:61, Mark 15:47, Luke 23:55, Matthew 16:21, Matthew 27:62-66, Matthew 28:1-15, Mark 16:1-11, Luke 24:1-12, John 20:1-18, Matthew 28:6, Mark 16:6, Luke 24:6, John 20:9, John 20:20, Luke 24:45, Mark 16:16-20

REFLECT

How did Jesus come to be buried in a rich man's tomb?

_____

_____

_____

Why were Joseph of Arimathea and Nicodemus making a significant sacrifice in burying Jesus' body?

_____

_____

_____

Why did the chief priests think they were in control of the events surrounding Jesus' burial?

_____

_____

_____

Why should we not be concerned that each of the four Gospels contains slightly different details of the resurrection?

_____

_____

_____

REMEMBER

It is impossible for us to see how God's plan will unfold. No one standing at the foot of Jesus' cross that day could have conceived that His body would be placed in the tomb a rich man had prepared for himself. But God's plan always comes to fruition. Joseph of Arimathea was a good man who was a secret follower of Jesus, and because the Sabbath was quickly approaching, he placed Jesus' body in his own tomb. God used Joseph to fulfill a prophecy.

Both Joseph of Arimathea and Nicodemus were wealthy, prominent men who were members of the Sanhedrin. By giving Jesus a proper burial, they were openly showing their belief in Him. They were endangering their positions within the Council and very likely faced other consequences as well.

The chief priests thought they had covered all the bases. They knew where Jesus' body had been laid, they convinced Pilate not only to place his official seal on the tomb but to station guards there as well. The priests were certain that no one could go into the tomb. But there was nothing they could do to prevent Jesus from coming *out* of the tomb.

The details of the resurrection vary slightly among the Gospel accounts. These variations do not imply contradictions. They imply only that each writer reported events from his own perspective as they related to his intended audience. The major event that occurred that morning is consistently told by all four: Jesus Christ is alive!

Seeking Son Light

Section 3
The Life of Christ

Lesson 10
Our Great Commission

The gospel message must never be watered down. Even though it is difficult for a person to hear that his lifestyle will send him to hell, it needs to be said.

Section 3:   The Life of Christ
Lesson 10:   Our Great Commission

> "Go therefore and make disciples of all the nations, baptizing them in the name of the Father and the Son and the Holy Spirit, teaching them to observe all that I commanded you; and lo, I am with you always, even to the end of the age."
>
> *(Matthew 28:19-20)*

With these words, which have come to be known as The Great Commission, Jesus ascended to heaven (Luke 24:51). He had given the Apostles their marching orders. But because they had not yet received the indwelling Holy Spirit, they surely thought the mission was daunting if not impossible.

But all things are possible with God (Mark 10:27) and we have the benefit of history to tell us that the Apostles did their jobs. According to the Pew Forum on Religion and Public Life, as of 2010 there were 2.18 billion Christians worldwide. That is around one-third of the global population. In the United States, 78% of adults claim to be Christians. Although only the Lord knows the heart condition of those claiming to be Christians, most conservative evangelical scholars believe the number of truly born-again Christians is far less than 78%.

Does that mean then that our work is done? Today there are over 6 billion humans living on the earth. Based on the statistics shown above, well over 4 billion people are living in spiritual darkness. No, our work is not done.

However, many Christians are not prepared for the task. Perhaps they have become confused about what the true gospel message is. Maybe they are afraid they will be embarrassed. But while Christians today are trying to get the knowledge and find the courage to tell others about Jesus Christ, people are dying.

What Every Christian Must Know

Our God is a Triune God. He is one God but exists in three persons: God the Father, God the Son and God the Holy Spirit. All three persons are equal in essence, power, intellect, emotion and will.

Sin separates us from God (Isaiah 59:2). Sin is anything that is contrary to the character of God. God is righteous and holy (Deuteronomy 32:4). Through the free will God had given them, Adam and Eve chose to sin (Genesis 3:1-8) and as a result, died spiritually and received a sinful nature. This sinful nature is an inherited trait and every human being ever born has been born with a sinful nature (Romans 5:12). If a person does not believe he has sinned, it is simply because he does not know God or His perfect character. We are all sinners (Romans 3:10).

The only way for us to achieve fellowship with God is for our sins to be forgiven. Having fellowship with God allows us to have a relationship with Him and to ensure that we will spend eternity with Him in heaven. On his own, man is incapable of removing sin from his life. He is in bondage to sin (John 8:34) from the moment of his birth and is helpless to pull himself away from sin's ironclad grasp.

The only way to receive forgiveness of our sin is through the shedding of blood (Hebrews 9:22). God will forgive sin only through the shedding of the blood of a perfect sacrifice. What is the perfect sacrifice? It is the life of a perfect and sinless human being. But all humans are born with a sinful nature and are incapable of perfection and sinlessness. Without the intervention of God, no one can be saved from sin.

Jesus Christ stepped up to be our Savior (John 1:29). Being the Second Person of the Trinity, Jesus is God (Colossians 1:15) and God is sinless (1 John 3:5).

In order to bring that sinlessness to humanity, God the Son became fully human while still remaining fully God
(John 10:30).

He was born into a poor Jewish family and lived a perfect, sinless life, qualifying Himself to be the perfect sacrifice to remove human sin (1 John 2:2).

Jesus allowed Himself to be sacrificed, shedding His perfect blood so we can have life with God. He was crucified, buried and raised again to life on the third day (1 Corinthians 15:3-4). We can be confident that the same power that raised Christ from the dead will raise us as well.

We can obtain forgiveness of our sins when we recognize our need for a Savior and place our faith in Christ.

(Ephesians 2:8-9)

We must decide to turn away from our sins and turn toward Christ. This action of turning away from one thing and turning toward another is called "repentance"; it goes hand-in-hand with placing our faith in Christ and it is required for salvation (Luke 13:3).

Through His grace, God opens our eyes and changes our hearts (2 Corinthians 3:15-16). Once called, we begin to see our sin the way God sees our sin and we finally understand our need for a Savior. We recognize our hopeless situation and acknowledge that we are powerless against the mastery of sin in our lives (Colossians 1:13-14).

We must make the conscious and deliberate decision to trust what the Bible says about who Jesus Christ is and what He has made available for us. *This* is the decision to turn away from sin and turn toward Christ. This decision *must* be unshakeable. He is trustworthy and faithful and He will not fail us.

In addition to forgiveness of our sins, we receive the gift of the Holy Spirit. When we come to Christ for salvation, He sends the Holy Spirit to dwell within us (Romans 8:9). With the help of the Holy Spirit, we have the strength to turn away from our sins and live the kind of life God wants us to live.

Because of our love for God and His saving grace, we want Jesus Christ to live through us and use us to tell sinners throughout the world about the availability of His gift of salvation.

<u>The Problem with the Modern Gospel</u>

The Apostle Paul admonished the Galatians for listening to "a different gospel" (Galatians 1:6-8). Paul knew there was no other gospel than the one he received directly from Jesus Christ. If false teachings were a problem during the time of the Apostles, how much more of a problem is it for today's church?

The modern gospel message tells people that Jesus wants above all else for them to be happy and fulfilled. He wants them to have happy marriages, perfect children and satisfying work. His primary mission in coming to earth was to bring peace and joy.

Evangelists who preach this message are often more concerned with filling seats in their auditoriums than in filling heaven with true believers. They are often passionate in their teaching and truly believe they are sharing the authentic gospel. But they have allowed themselves to be deceived; they have wandered away from the truth of God's Word and they will be judged for their choices (2 Peter 2:1-3). If their teaching, in whole or in part, cannot stand up to the scrutiny of God's Word, then it must not be taught. And just as the teachers must remain in the Word, so must their hearers. If a teaching does not have its foundation in the Word of God, it must be thrown out.

God's Word, the Bible, tells us everything we need to know in order to detect the lies.

This is the challenge facing born-again Christians today who want to share the one true gospel with these lost and deceived people. The problem is that those who have heard this modern gospel are feeling so good about themselves as a result of the lies they have been told, they do not believe they need a Savior.

Our Great Commission

Ray Comfort is a modern evangelist who uses an ancient method for sharing the true gospel. It is the same method used by Jesus and the Apostles. That is, he uses the Law, and more specifically the Ten Commandments, to reveal the sins of the people.

Ask a person if he has ever stolen anything and he will probably say that he has. Ask him if he has ever told a lie, even a tiny white lie, and again, he will probably admit to that sin. But in his way of thinking, he doesn't believe it will keep him out of heaven; he doesn't think he has a problem. And *that is* the problem. People today, even people who regularly attend church, do not see sin the way God sees sin. And until people recognize that sin is vile and filthy to God, they tend to believe that their spiritual condition is just fine.

John MacArthur says, "We need to adjust our presentation of the gospel. We cannot dismiss the fact that God hates sin and punishes sinners with eternal torment. How can we begin a gospel presentation by telling people on their way to hell that God has a wonderful plan for their lives?"

In July 1741, preacher Jonathan Edwards was invited to speak at a church in Enfield, Connecticut. The pastor of that church knew his congregation was unmoved by the gospel message and in spite of his own efforts, he could not make them recognize the seriousness of their sin. Edwards delivered what is possibly the most famous sermon ever given. It was called, "Sinners in the Hands of an Angry God." He used vivid imagery to describe man's lost condition and the fierceness of God's wrath. By the time he finished giving the sermon, the people in the congregation were groaning, crying and begging to be told how what they could do to be saved.

Even today, more than 250 years after the sermon was first given, it stands as one of the greatest calls to repentance the church has ever seen. This is the type of evangelism we need today to correct the damage done by the preaching of the modern gospel.

What Can We Do?

Let's face it: not everyone is cut out to be an evangelist. The thought of approaching strangers on a street to share the gospel can be terrifying. But when we use the spiritual gifts God has given us, we cannot fail. One way that every Christian can evangelize is to live out his faith. Be verbal about being a Christian and then live out the Christian life every day. Our actions often speak louder than words and people are watching.

We always need to be prepared to defend and share the gospel when opportunities present themselves (1 Peter 3:15). People must be given the facts about the gospel in a way that is easy for them to understand.

> # The gospel message must never be watered down. Even though it is difficult for a person to hear that his lifestyle will send him to hell, it needs to be said.

Encourage people to read the Bible. That is the only way they can come to know God's character and know what is pleasing to Him. The more time they spend in the Bible, the better they will know what God expects of them (1 Timothy 4:13).

Eternal life is real. But not everyone will experience eternal life in Paradise in fellowship with God (Matthew 25:46). Only those who have accepted Jesus Christ as their Savior will experience that. Getting into heaven is like trying to get into an exclusive country club. You either have to pay a lot of money or you have to know someone who will sponsor you. Since there is not enough money or valuables in the entire universe to buy one's way into heaven, the only option is to know someone who can get you in. When you know Jesus, the door to eternal life is opened.

Understand that the job of a Christian is to give the true, original, undiluted gospel message to unbelievers. People must be told that God will judge them. He will not simply give them a wink and a nod and ignore their sin. Unbelievers must hear the gospel message from believers. But once that message is given, it is the Holy Spirit who works in the unbeliever's life to convict him of his sin. The unbeliever will either choose to accept the truth or reject it. As believers, we need to be faithful to plant the seed of truth and then allow the Holy Spirit tend its growth.

Thank God daily for the blessings He has brought into your life. Ask Him to give you the wisdom and courage to speak out for Him and to give understanding to those you reach out to. And above all, thank Him for choosing you.

LESSON 10 – SUMMARY

READ

Matthew 28:19-20, Luke 24:51, Mark 10:27, Isaiah 59:2, Deuteronomy 32:4, Genesis 3:1-8, Romans 5:12, Romans 3:10, John 8:34, Hebrews 9:22, John 1:29, Colossians 1:15, 1 John 3:5, John 10:30, 1 John 2:2, 1 Corinthians 15:3-4, Ephesians 2:8-9, Luke 13:3, 2 Corinthians 3:15-16, Colossians 1:13-14, Romans 8:9, Galatians 1:6-8, 2 Peter 2:1-3, 1 Peter 3:15, 1 Timothy 4:13, Matthew 25:46

REFLECT

What separates us from God and how can we have fellowship with Him?

_____

_____

_____

What is required for the forgiveness of sins?

_____

_____

_____

What did Jesus Christ accomplish for us that no other human being could accomplish?

_____

_____

_____

What is one way every Christian can evangelize?

_____

_____

_____

If we are faithful to plant the seed of truth in the hearts of unbelievers, who tends its growth?

_____

_____

_____

REMEMBER

Sin separates us from God and the only way we can have fellowship with Him is through the forgiveness of our sins.

The shedding of blood is required for the forgiveness of sins. The blood of animals will not remove sin. Only the blood of a perfect and sinless human being has the power to do that. Jesus Christ led a perfect and sinless life and He allowed Himself to be sacrificed for us.

Jesus Christ was not born with a sinful nature like we are. So while He was fully human, He was also fully God and He was able to live a perfect, sinless life. No other human being would ever be able to accomplish that.

In order to achieve forgiveness of our sins and spend eternity in heaven with God we must acknowledge our need for a Savior and turn away from our sin.

The problem with the modern gospel is that it does not teach people God's true nature and our need for repentance. It does not teach about God's eternal judgment on those who reject Jesus Christ. It tells people that God wants only for them to be happy and to have perfect lives here on earth. It makes people feel so good about themselves, they do not think they need a Savior.

One way every Christian can evangelize is to live out his faith. We must allow others to see how the Holy Spirit has changed our lives from the inside out.

As Christians, our job is to tell unbelievers the truth of the gospel. Those who hear will either accept the truth or reject it. There is nothing we can do as mere men to cause a person to change the condition of his heart. Only the Holy Spirit can do that.

Seeking Son Light
Section 3
The Life of Christ

For further reading...

"Jesus, a Theography" by Leonard Sweet and Frank Viola

"The Darkness and the Dawn" by Charles Swindoll

"The Day Jesus Died" by Jim Bishop

"The School of Biblical Evangelism" by Ray Comfort and Kirk Cameron

"The New Evidence that Demands a Verdict" by Josh McDowell

"The Case for the Resurrection of Jesus" by Gary Habermas

"Sinners in the Hands of an Angry God" by Jonathan Edwards

"The Power of the Blood of Christ" by Andrew Murray

About the Author

Rebecca Helton has enjoyed a long career in the banking industry. She and her husband Ron live near Springfield, Illinois.

CPSIA information can be obtained at www.ICGtesting.com
Printed in the USA
LVOW07s1018240816

501548LV00001B/3/P